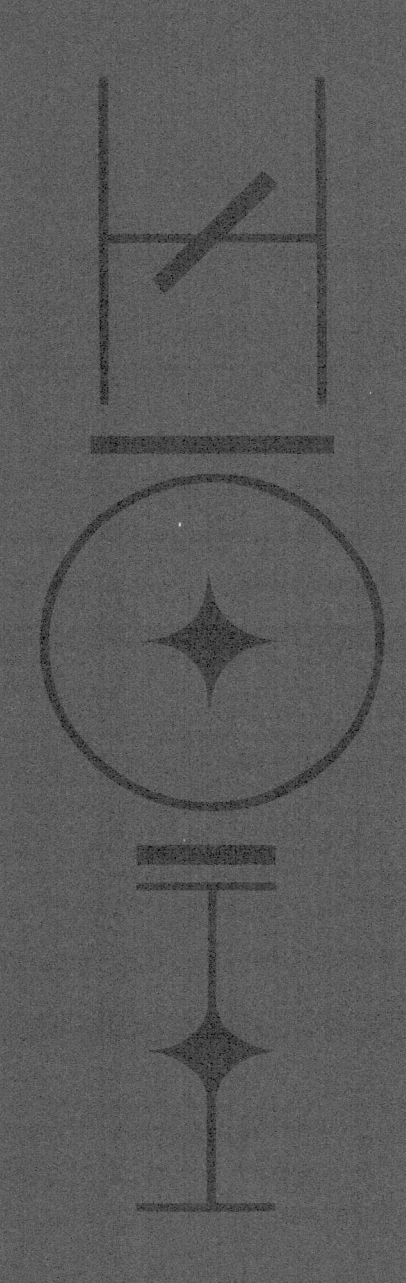

This Journal Belongs To:

INNER MAGIC

A Journal for Tapping into Your Intuition

ALEX NARANJO & MARLENE VARGAS

FOUNDERS OF THE HOUSE OF INTUITION

Clarkson Potter/Publishers
New York

ARE YOU READY?

ARE YOU READY?

✦

Think of this book not as a journal but as a journey. The intention of this journey is to help usher you from where (and perhaps who) you are right now to where (and perhaps who) you want and were meant to be.

It's not about changing anything that's "wrong" with you, but about leading you toward what is most right and allowing you the opportunity to demonstrate to yourself how deeply powerful you already are and how supported you are in every moment of every day. It's a practice of letting go of what no longer serves you and bringing in what does. It's about making the time to get quiet and turn inward, to hear your own voice, your own guidance, and your own intuition.

We always tell people that, *yes*! Magic is real and it works, and not only do we all have access to magic, but we *are* all magic (yes, you too!). *But* magic is about much more than just spellcasting. That right there is external magic. Inner magic—which is where all magic begins—is about being accountable by tapping into our own intuition, power, truth, and innate wisdom. As you can imagine, all of this takes some intentional work.

Welcome to the work.

When we do this work, our magic becomes even more inspired, more powerful, and more . . . well, magical. And that's exactly what these pages are designed to help you do. We hope you'll consider this your safe place and a sacred tool for an ongoing conversation with your soul, your higher self, your ancestors, your spirit guide, and the universe.

Most important, know that the only magic required in these pages is *you*. Simply by being here, by giving yourself the opportunity to be guided by intuition, by trusting your intuition to lead you to the page and question you need to consider in this moment, and by being present as you put pen to paper and intuitively and authentically answer that question, you are activating your magic and your connection with spirit, allowing it to come through and guide you.

HOW TO USE THIS JOURNAL

Among many other things, this journal is a practice of tapping into and trusting your intuition.

Your intuition is like a muscle. And just like any other muscle in your body, the more you use your intuition, the stronger it grows. The more you practice using your intuition, the more it will speak to you and the better you will become at recognizing it, hearing what it has to say, and not second-guessing those "hunches" and "niggles" that arise. As you practice using your intuition and then seeing those situations play out, you will begin to believe in your intuition more, recognize how powerful it is (and, by extension, how powerful you are), and understand that it's there to guide you.

BEFORE YOU BEGIN WRITING, light a candle or incense (preferably on your altar, if have one); take three slow, deep breaths; set an intention for your writing session; clear your mind of worldly concerns; and call upon your ancestors, spirit guide, the universe, spirit, or whomever resonates with you.

CLOSE YOUR EYES AND FLIP TO THE PAGE YOU FEEL CALLED TO, JUST LIKE YOU WOULD WITH ANY OTHER SORT OF ORACLE. Notice your reaction to the page you land on. Because we're using this journal as a sacred tool, it's going to give you the question that you need (though not necessarily the one you want). Does it eerily reflect precisely what's been on your mind or something you've been working on? Or do you feel resistant to sitting with the question? Either way, trust the process and move forward with the writing.

Because we've designed this journal to be used as an oracle rather than in a more linear fashion, you may find yourself drawn back to the same issue until you heal, solve, or evolve beyond it. Have you ever used a tarot deck and found that you draw the same card over and over again? The same applies here. Not only is it okay to draw the same question multiple times, but it's *meaningful*. It might be spirit's way of drawing your attention to how far you've come on a certain matter. It might be a reminder that there's still work to be done or an opportunity for you to get even stronger in a certain area of your life. It could be a certain ancestor's way of communicating with you. Only you know the answer, so it's up to you to tap into and understand why you're being called to a question.

IF YOUR INTUITION DRAWS YOU BACK TO A QUESTION YOU'VE ALREADY ANSWERED, HERE'S WHAT TO DO. First, notice your initial answer to the prompt. Then turn your attention to the space labeled "Reflection." This is a space where you can write about why you think you're drawn back to this question, how you feel about that, and how (or if) your thoughts have changed since you last wrote. Take the time to recognize how far you've come from the original answer, even if it doesn't feel like much time has passed. And if you haven't yet progressed or done work around this topic, you might write about why that is.

AFTER YOU'VE FINISHED YOUR WRITING FOR THE DAY, IT'S TIME TO RELEASE. Notice how you feel, particularly any feelings of heaviness or being stuck. Even though some of these questions may bring up some difficult, painful, or heavy memories or feelings, the intention is to process them (which you've now accomplished through your writing) so that you can release them. With that in mind, you might take yourself for a walk to move through feelings of being stuck—preferably somewhere in nature and barefoot to reconnect with Mother Earth. You can take a bath or shower, setting the intention to cleanse and shift your energy. Perhaps you might move some furniture around to shift the energy of the room you're in. Or, if it helps, you could even have a good cry and notice how you feel lighter and cleansed after.

We've also included some of our favorite, most time-tested mantras, affirmations, and (nondenominational) prayers throughout the book to support you along the way. Notice when one calls to you and perhaps even speak it aloud. There is power in using your voice to assert your worth, to express gratitude, and to call for support and guidance when you need it.

This entire writing ritual from beginning to end is a process of connecting with, shifting, and honing your inner magic. Use it daily, weekly, or whenever you feel called to it. Just as we use spellcasting to change, shift, and transmute the energy of the external world, you are doing the same to your inner world, to the magic in you.

LET'S GET STARTED . . .

After this initial question, you will follow your own unique path through these pages (until the final question in the journal, which you will answer once all of the other questions are complete). But first, let's all begin with this:

Set an intention.

WHAT DO I WANT TO MANIFEST ON MY JOURNEY THROUGH THIS JOURNAL?

Close your eye.

page you f

and flip to the

l called to.

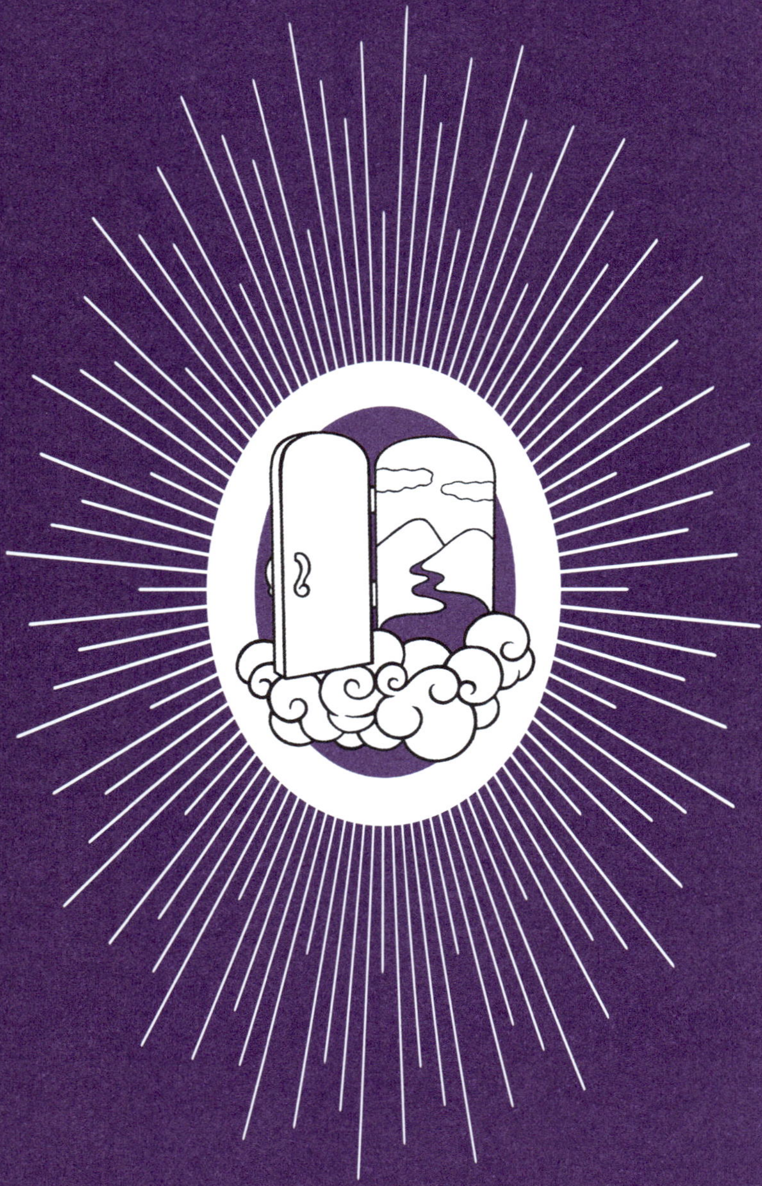

MY INTUITION GUIDES ME

✦

My intuition guides me. Through my intuition, I am connected to humanity and its glorious wonders. I make decisions based on my visions, not based on others' opinions about me. Others are attracted to me for my natural ability to connect with the outer world. I connect to my higher self by connecting to my inner magic. I am ready for my psychic ability to increase so I am attuned to myself and the forces that support me.

WHAT DO PEOPLE TELL ME ABOUT WHO I AM THAT ISN'T TRUE?

Date ___ / ___ / ___

Date _____ / _____ / _____

I release fear and ...

to guide me thr...

vite my intuition

gh to success.

WHAT PARTS OF MYSELF DO I FEEL LIKE I NEED TO HIDE?
WHAT PARTS OF MYSELF MIGHT I BE SUBCONSCIOUSLY HIDING?

Date ___/___/___

Date ___/___/___

IN WHAT AREAS OF MY LIFE DO I NEED CHANGE?

Date _____ / _____ / _____

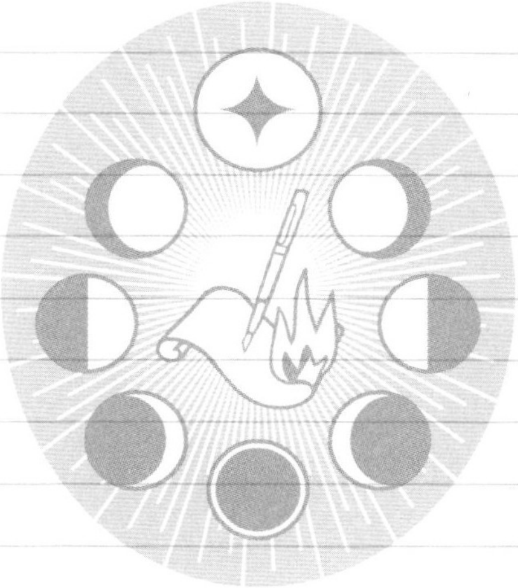

Date ____ / ____ / ____

WHAT AM I GRATEFUL FOR TODAY?

Date _____ / _____ / _____

Date _____ / _____ / _____

HOW MIGHT I PUSH MYSELF OUT OF MY COMFORT ZONE IN A HEALTHY WAY? WHAT MIGHT I GAIN, AND HOW MIGHT I GROW FROM DOING SO?

Date ___ / ___ / ___

Date ___ / ___ / ___

My passion

to my great

vill lead me

t potential.

WHAT MAKES ME HAPPY?

Date _____ / _____ / _____

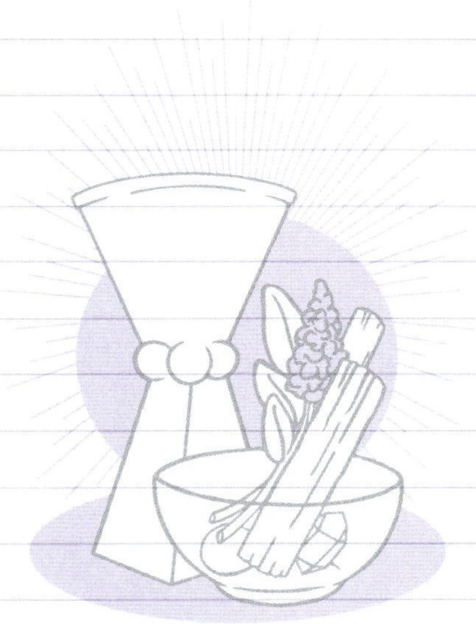

Date ____ / ____ / ____

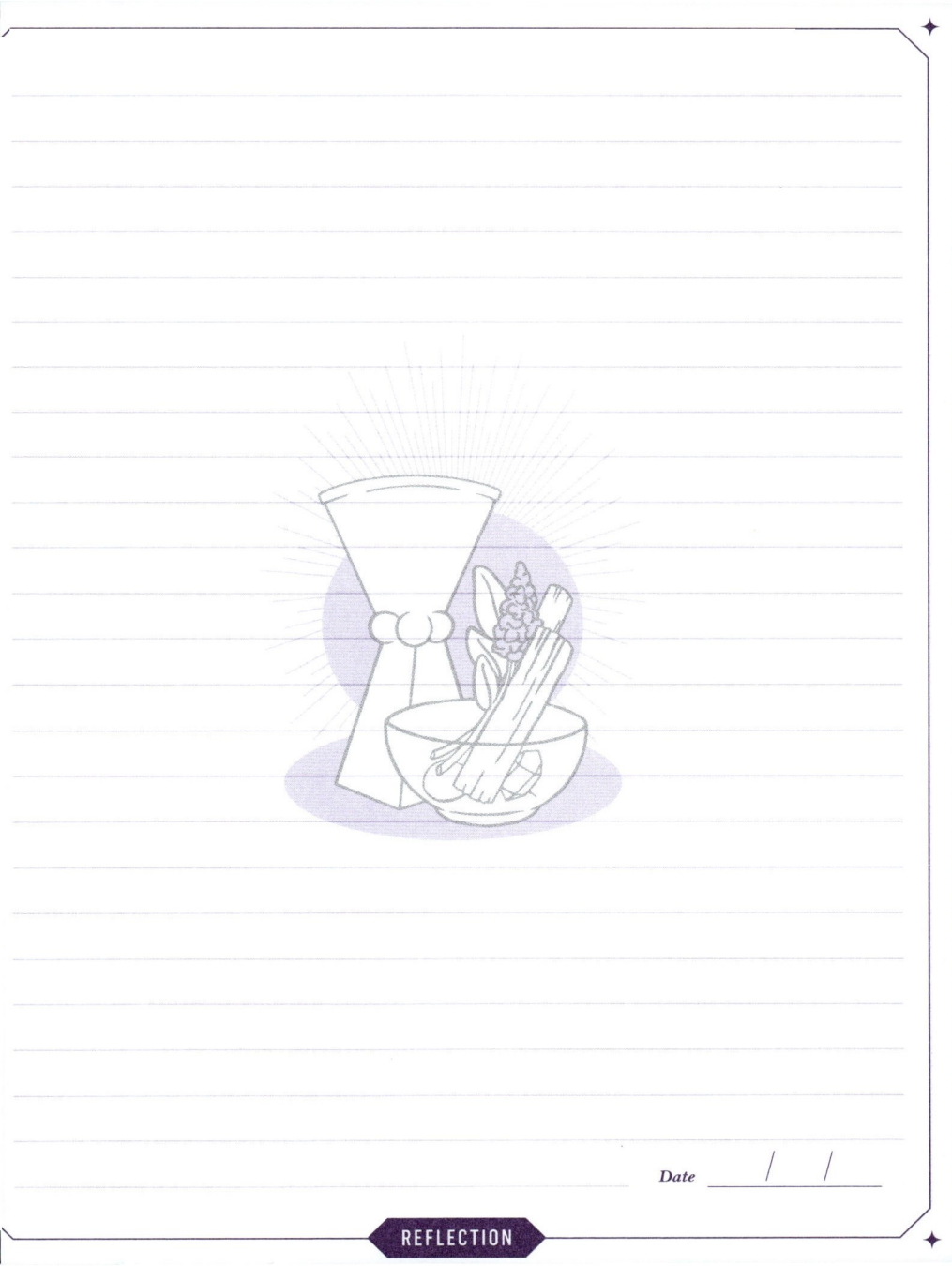

HOW CAN I HONOR MY BODY?

Date ___ / ___ / ___

Date _____ / _____ / _____

HOW DO I MANAGE DIFFICULT PERSONALITIES?
WHAT CAN I DO DIFFERENTLY THAT WILL BETTER SERVE ME?

Date _____ / _____ / _____

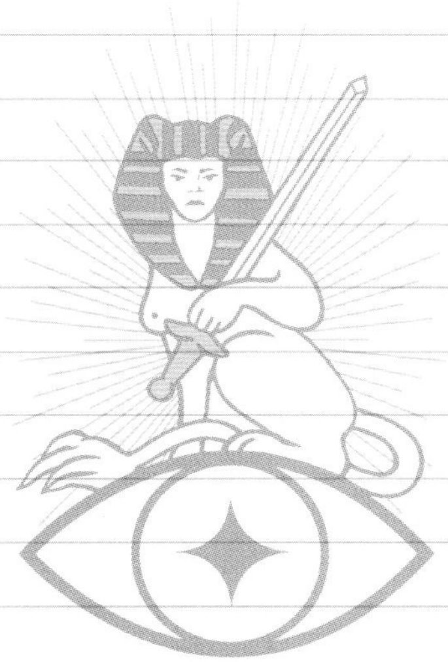

Date ___ / ___ / ___

HOW DO I FEEL ABOUT WHAT I SEE WHEN I LOOK IN THE MIRROR?

Date ___ / ___ / ___

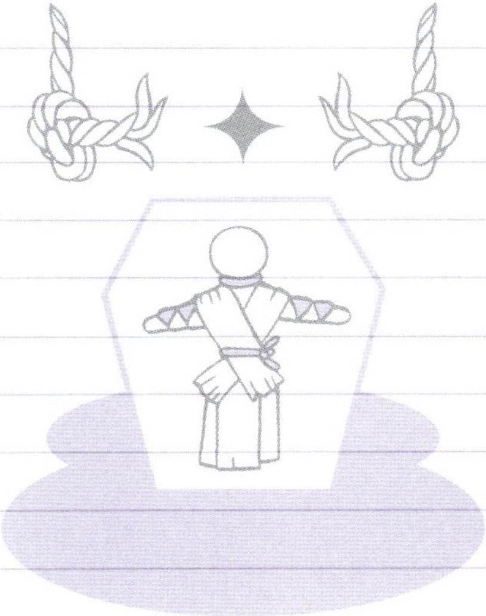

Date ___ / ___ / ___

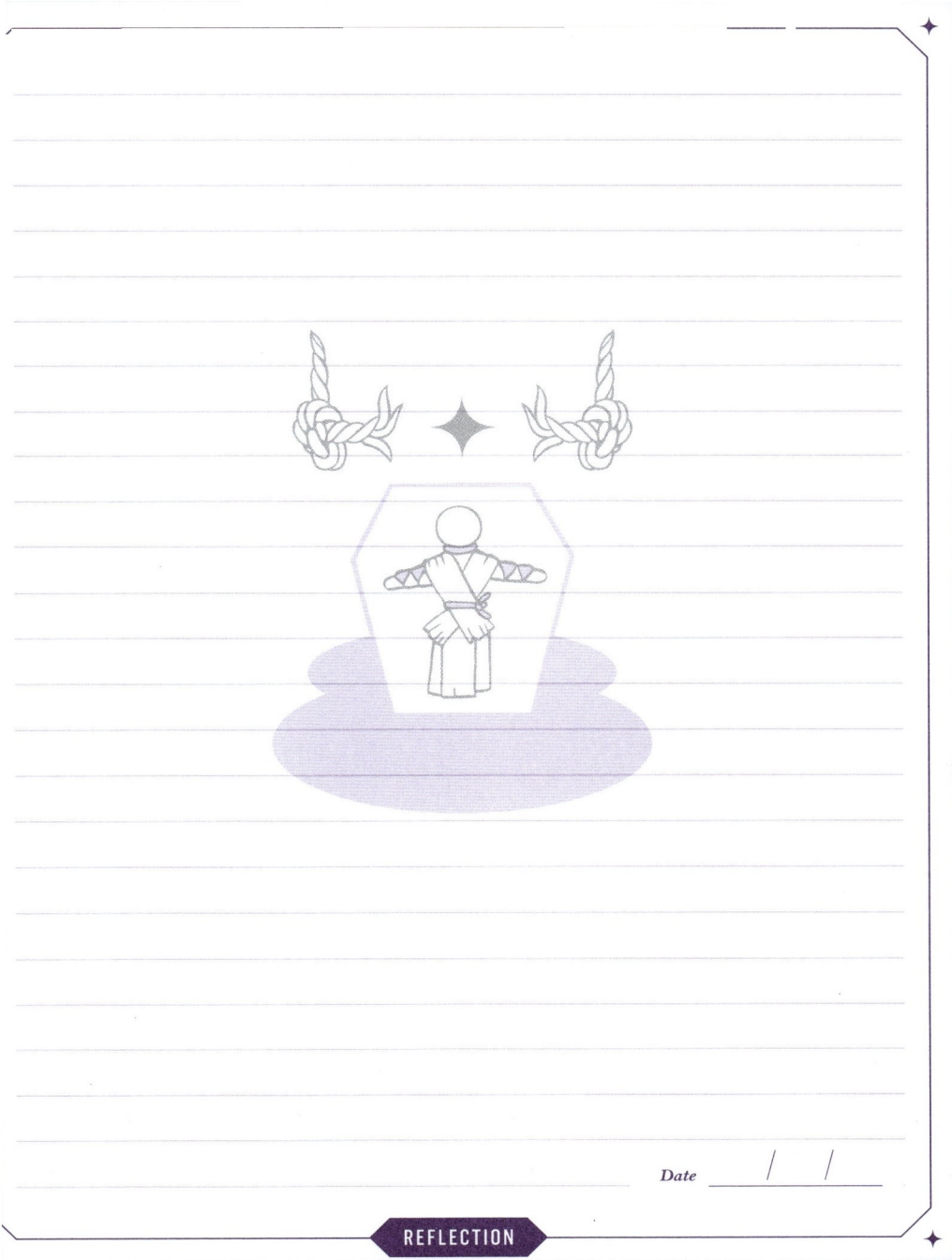

WHERE IN MY LIFE AM I CURRENTLY (OR HABITUALLY) HOLDING BACK?

Date _____ / _____ / _____

Date _____ / _____ / _____

HOW DOES MY IDEAL PARTNER MAKE ME FEEL?

Date ___ / ___ / ___

Date _____ / _____ / _____

HOW MUCH OF WHAT OTHERS THINK MATTERS TO ME?
DO I WANT IT TO MATTER MORE OR LESS THAN IT DOES RIGHT NOW?

Date ___ / ___ / ___

Date _____ / _____ / _____

WHAT CHALLENGING EXPERIENCE OR SITUATION
DO I STILL NEED TO LEARN FROM?

Date _____ / _____ / _____

Date ___/___/___

AM I LIVING IN MY TRUTH? IN WHAT WAYS?

Date ___/___/___

Date _____ / _____ / _____

WHAT ARE MY BELIEFS ABOUT MONEY?
HOW MIGHT THEY BE HOLDING ME BACK?

Date _____ / ____ / ____

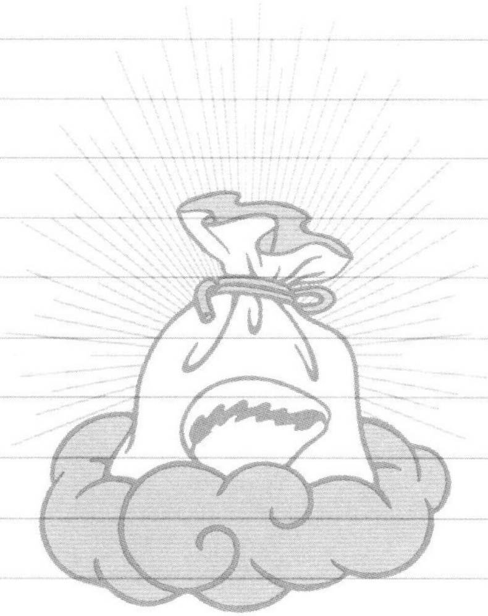

Date / /

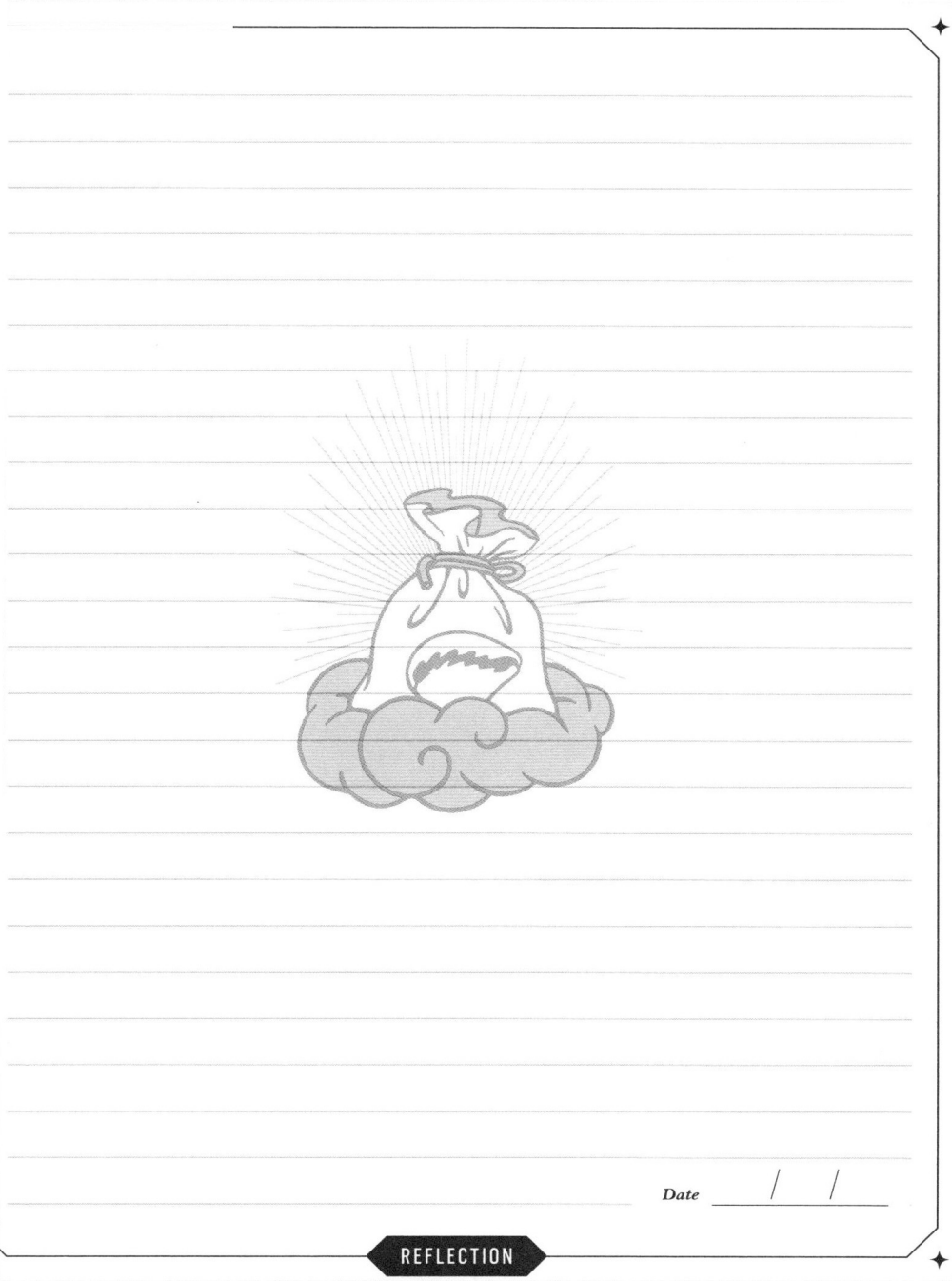

WHAT IS STANDING IN THE WAY OF ME BEING MY BEST SELF?
HOW MIGHT I SHIFT THIS?

Date _____ / ___ / ___

Date ___/___/___

I am a phoenix. ...

with newfound

awareness of

ise from the ashes

trength and full

ry great power.

WHAT ANCESTOR DO I WANT TO GIVE THANKS TO AND WHY?

Date ___/___/___

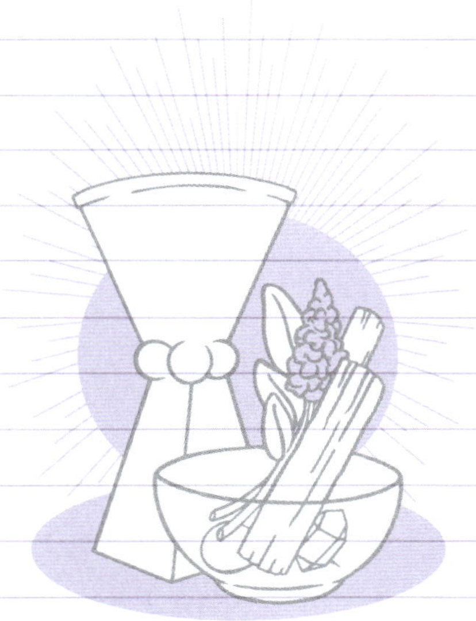

Date ___ / ___ / ___

WHAT IS A TIME WHEN SOMEONE LEFT A POSITIVE IMPRESSION ON ME? HOW DID THIS MAKE ME FEEL?

Date _____ / _____ / _____

Date _____ / _____ / _____

WHAT AM I AFRAID TO LET GO OF AND WHY?

Date ___ / ___ / ___

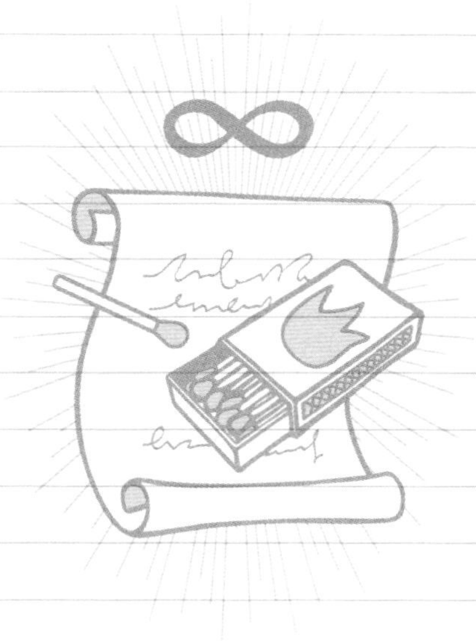

Date / /

DO I FEEL FINANCIALLY SECURE?
WHAT AREAS CAN USE IMPROVEMENT AND HOW?

Date _____ / _____ / _____

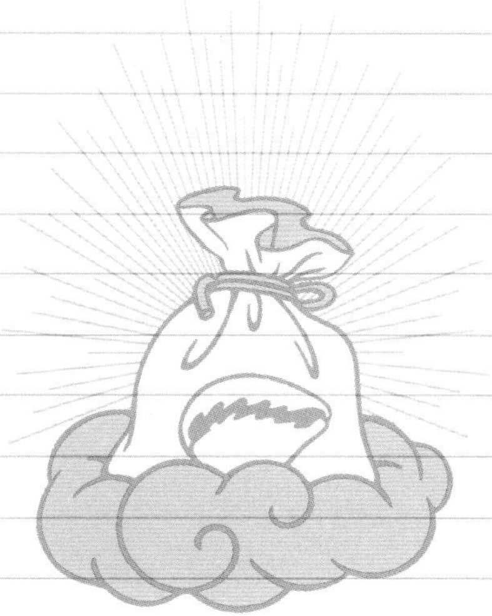

Date ____ / ____ / ____

REFLECTION

WHAT DOES SELF-LOVE MEAN TO ME?

Date _____ / _____ / _____

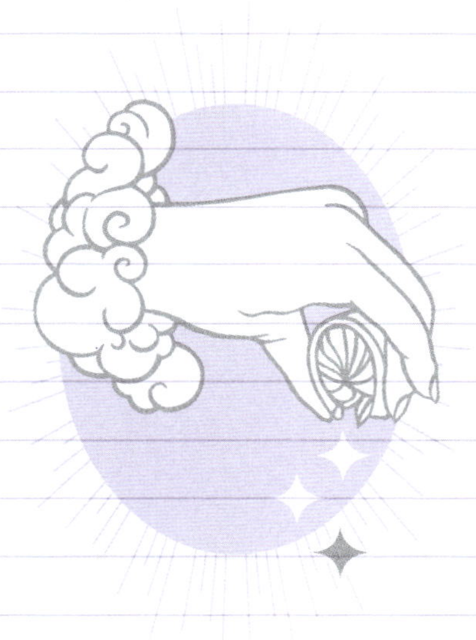

Date / /

IS THERE A MESSAGE I NEED TO TELL SOMEONE?

Date _____ / _____ / _____

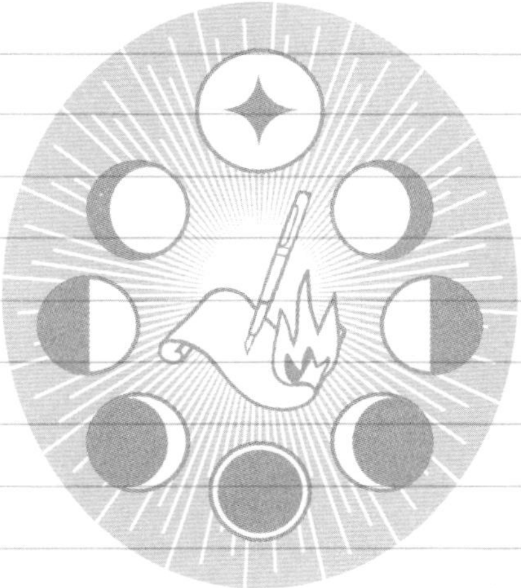

Date ____/____/____

My soul's evol

heights as I take m

from the shado

ion reaches new

elf and humanity

into the light.

WHAT IS MY FAVORITE SEASON OF THE YEAR? WHY?

Date ___/___/___

Date ___/___/___

HOW DO I CONNECT WITH SPIRIT?

Date _____ / _____ / _____

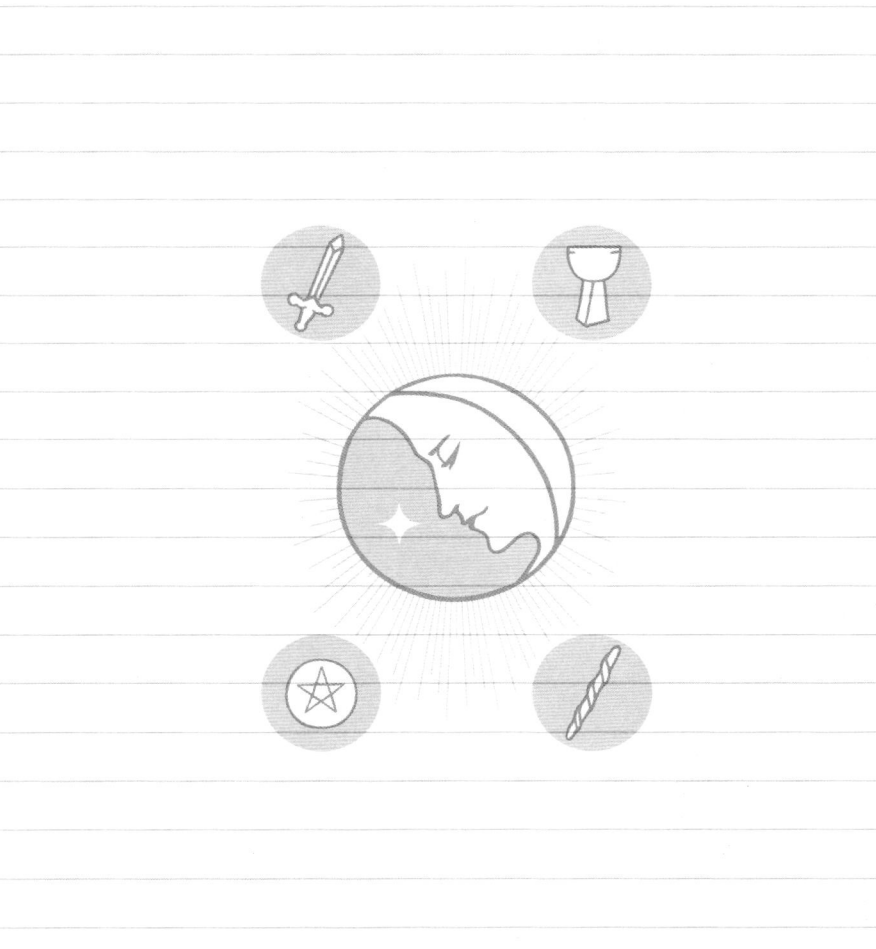

Date _____/_____/_____

IN WHAT AREA OF MY LIFE DO I FEEL THE MOST SCARCITY?

Date _____ / _____ / _____

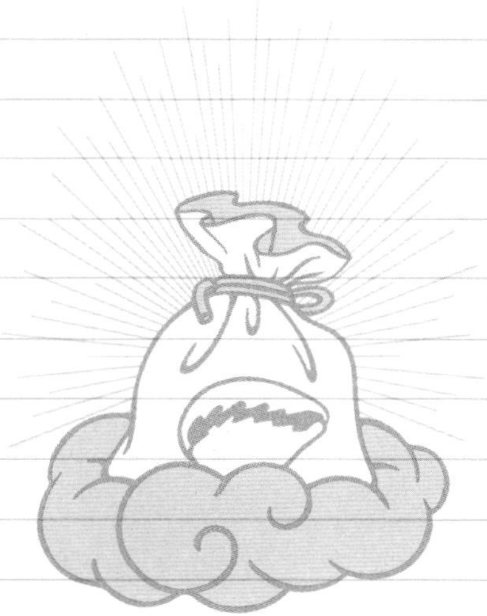

Date / /

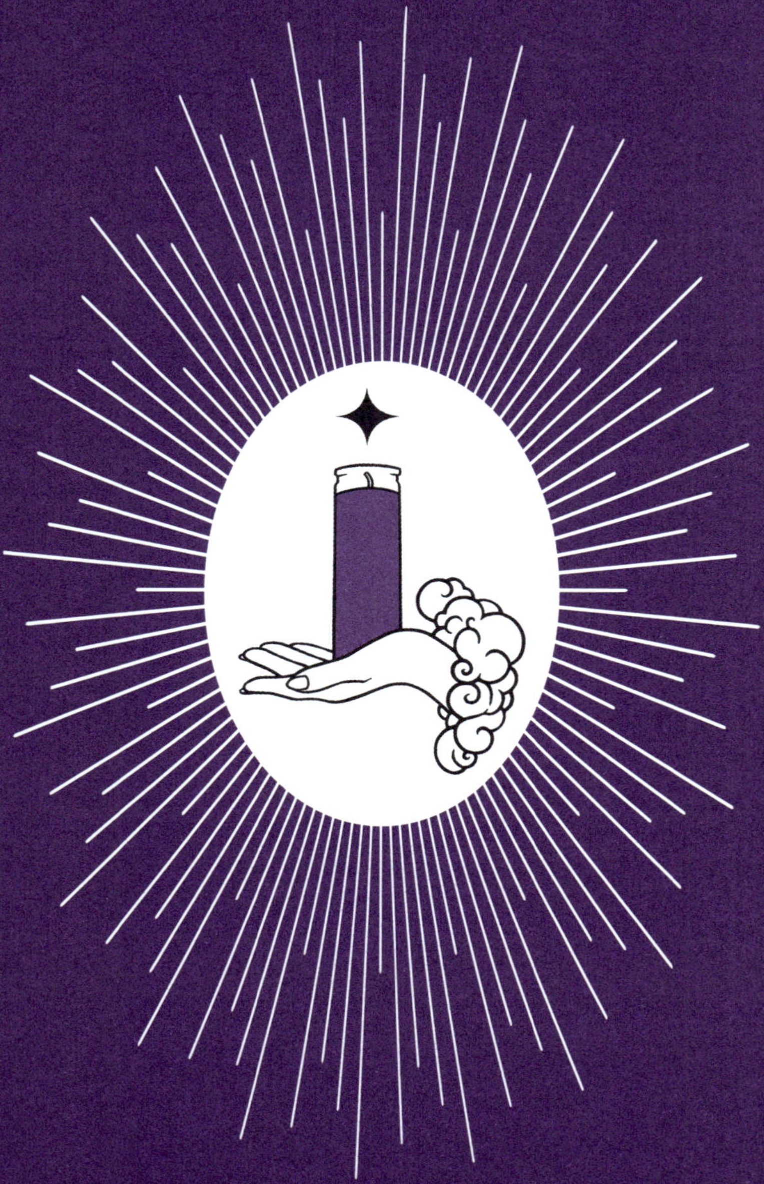

AS I REAWAKEN

✦

I take action as I enter into this reawakening of self.
I use my strength to push through any obstacle in my path.
The more I focus on my inner riches, the more happiness
I manifest in my spiritual wellspring.

AM I TAKING ANYTHING OR ANYONE FOR GRANTED?

Date ___ / ___ / ___

Date _____ / _____ / _____

WHAT DOES "FAMILY" MEAN TO ME?

Date ___/___/___

Date _____ / _____ / _____

I am a seeker. I w[...]

with steadiness a[...]

full of growth[...]

...k toward my goals

...envision a future

...d opportunity.

WHO DO I NEED TO LET GO OF? WHY HAVEN'T I DONE SO YET?

Date _____ / _____ / _____

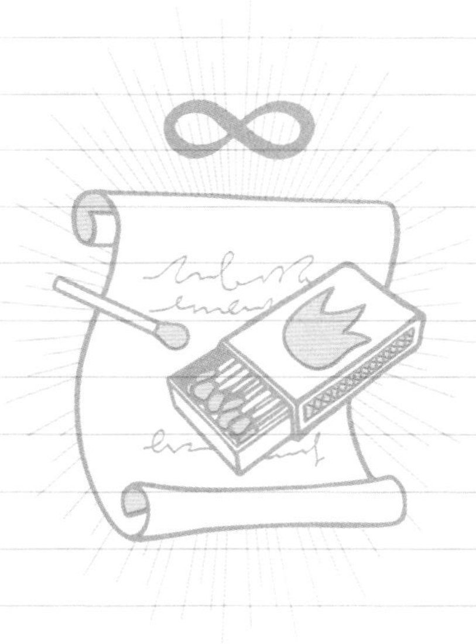

Date ___/___/___

IF I COULD CHANGE ONE THING ABOUT MY LIFE, WHAT WOULD IT BE?

Date _____ / _____ / _____

Date ___/___/___

WHAT DO I DO TO TAKE CARE OF MYSELF
EMOTIONALLY, PHYSICALLY, AND SPIRITUALLY?

Date _____ / _____ / _____

Date ___/___/___

IN WHAT AREAS HAVE I BEEN TOO STRICT WITH MYSELF?
WHAT DOES THIS LOOK LIKE?

Date _____ / _____ / _____

Date _____/_____/_____

WHAT IS MY FAVORITE TRAIT ABOUT MYSELF?

Date _____ / _____ / _____

REFLECTION

WHAT CAN I DO TO BE HEARD?

Date _____ / _____ / _____

Date _____ / _____ / _____

IF I CONTINUE LIVING MY LIFE JUST AS I AM TODAY, WHAT WILL MY GREATEST REGRET BE?

Date ___/___/___

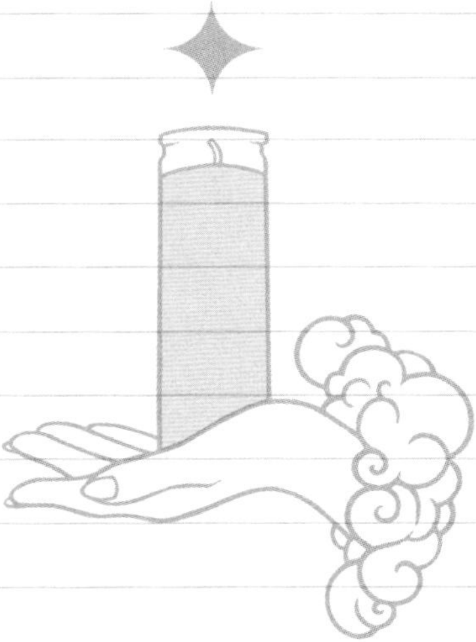

Date ___ / ___ / ___

WAS THERE A TIME MY SPIRIT GUIDE CONNECTED WITH ME?
HOW DID IT FEEL? IF I HAVEN'T FELT A CONNECTION WITH MY SPIRIT GUIDE,
WAS THERE A MOMENT WHEN I WISHED FOR THAT KIND OF CONNECTION,
AND WHAT DID I WANT FROM IT?

Date _____ / _____ / _____

Date ___ / ___ / ___

WHAT OR WHO AM I GIVING UNNECESSARY ENERGY AND ATTENTION TO?

Date _____ / _____ / _____

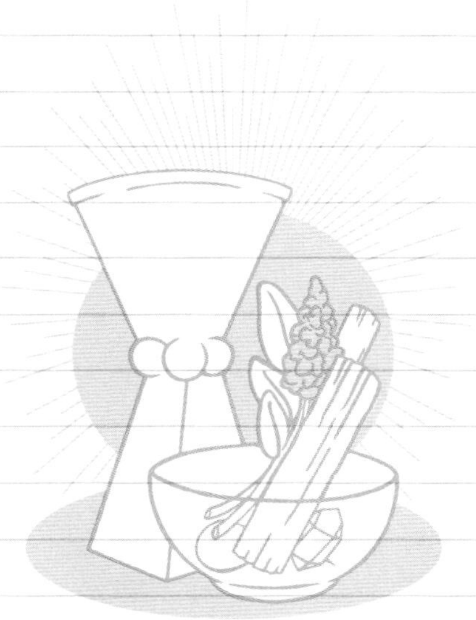

Date / /

HOW DOES MY FAMILY AFFECT MY MENTAL HEALTH
IN POSITIVE AND NEGATIVE WAYS?

Date ___/___/___

Date ___ / ___ / ___

WHAT MAKES ME FEEL ANXIOUS?
WHERE DO I FEEL IT IN MY BODY, AND WHAT DOES IT FEEL LIKE?

Date _____ / _____ / _____

Date ___/___/___

The cosmic messe

I travel through

of the cosmo

again a

er lives within me.

e energetic layers

o find myself

again.

HOW DOES MY INTUITION SPEAK TO ME?
IN WHAT WAYS DO I ACTIVELY STRENGTHEN MY INTUITION?

Date ___/___/___

Date ___ / ___ / ___

HOW DO I DISTINGUISH WHETHER MY EGO
OR HIGHER SELF IS SPEAKING TO ME?

Date ___ / ___ / ___

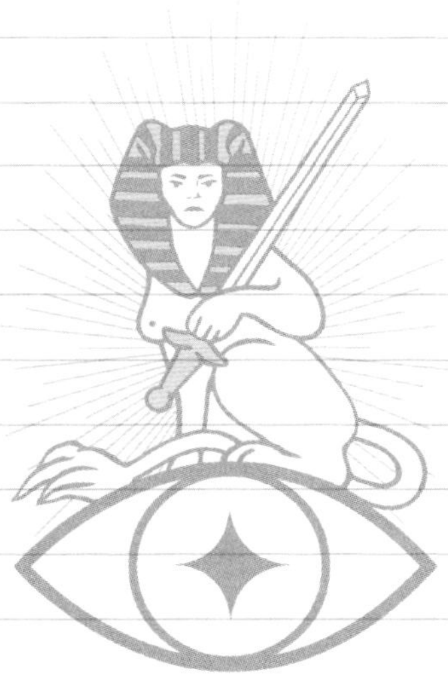

Date / /

IN WHAT AREAS HAVE I BEEN TOO LENIENT WITH MYSELF? HOW?

Date _____ / _____ / _____

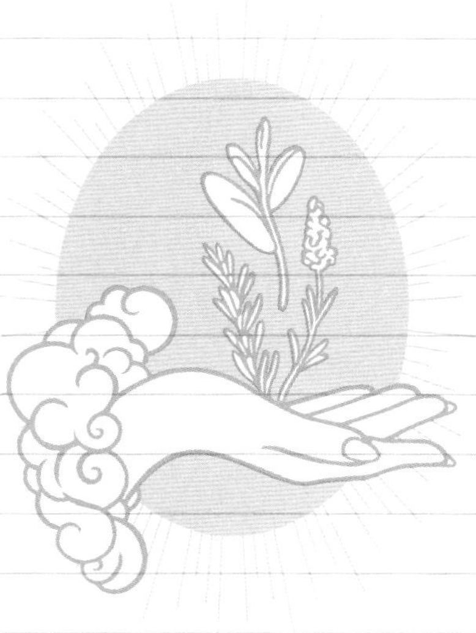

Date ___ / ___ / ___

REFLECTION

WHAT CHILDHOOD MEMORY HAS LEFT A POSITIVE IMPRESSION ON ME, AND HOW DOES IT IMPACT MY LIFE AND/OR BEHAVIOR?

Date _____ / _____ / _____

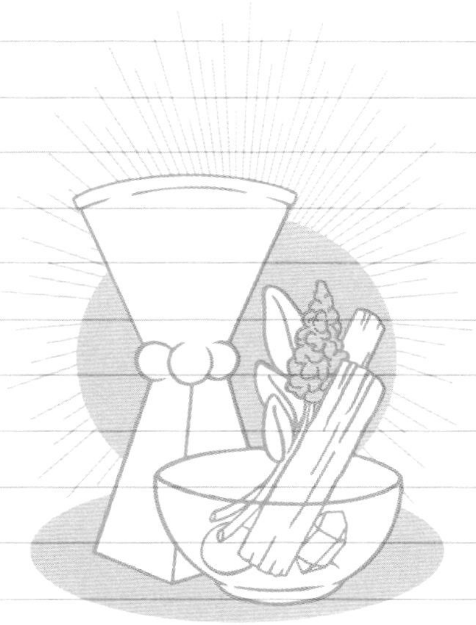

Date / /

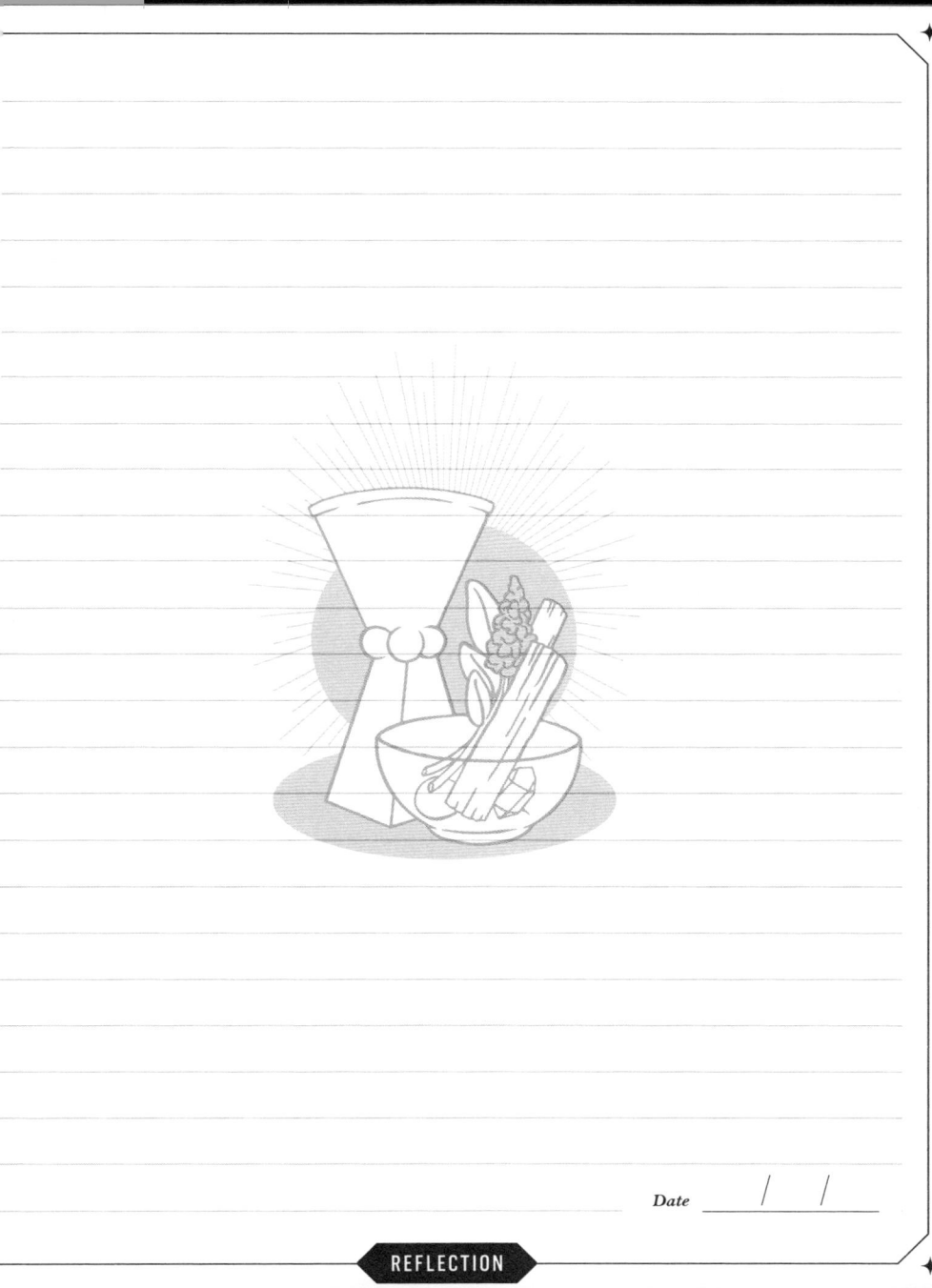

HOW DOES WHERE I FALL IN THE LINE OF SIBLINGS—OLDEST, MIDDLE, YOUNGEST, OR ONLY CHILD—AFFECT HOW I RELATE TO FAMILY LIFE?

Date _____ / _____ / _____

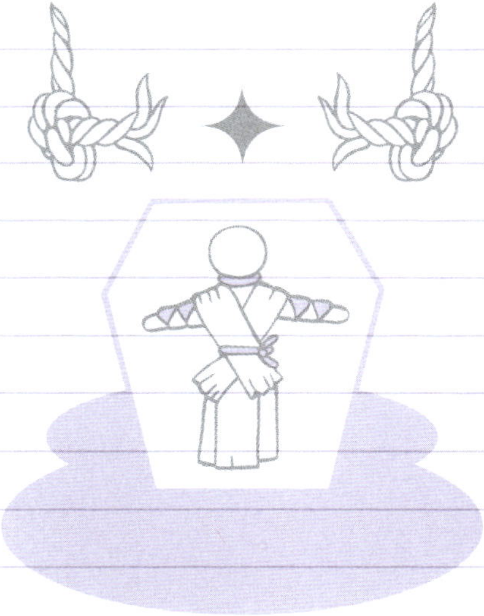

Date / /

HOW DO THE UNIVERSE AND/OR MY ANCESTORS
SPEAK TO ME THROUGH SIGNS?

Date _____ / _____ / _____

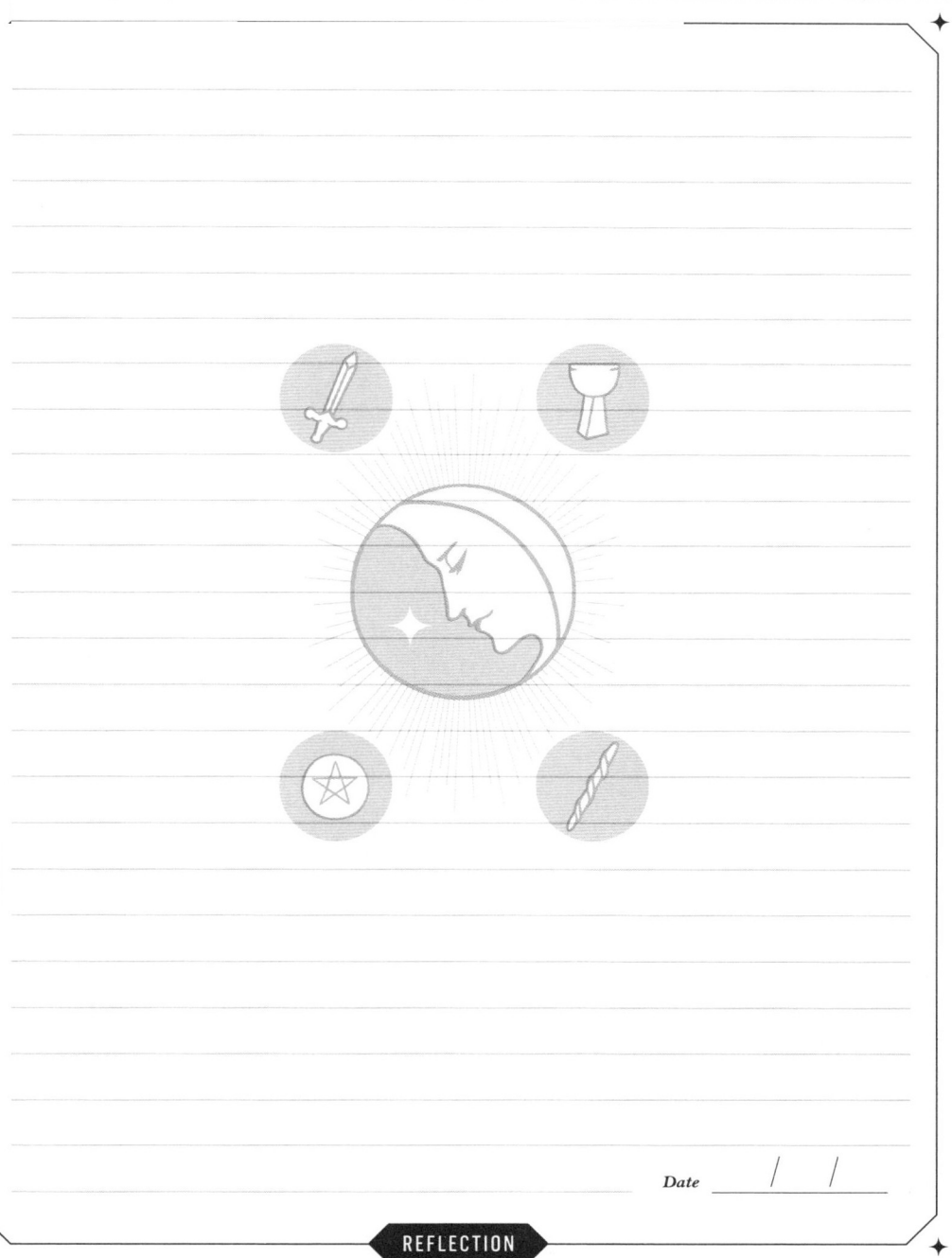

Date _____ / ___ / _____

WHAT IS THE MOST SPIRITUALLY POWERFUL EXPERIENCE I'VE EVER HAD, AND HOW DID IT IMPACT MY LIFE?

Date ___/___/___

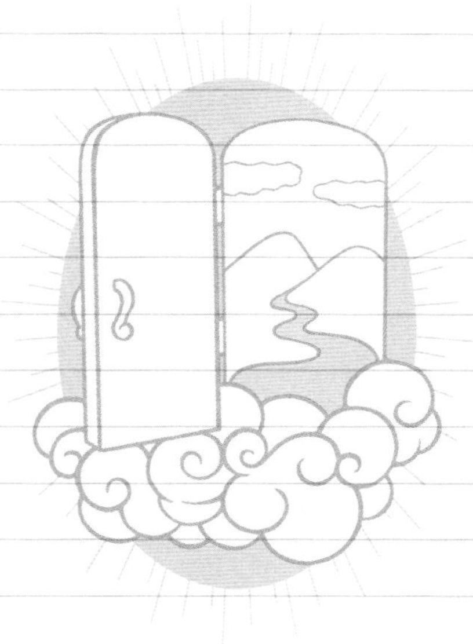

Date / /

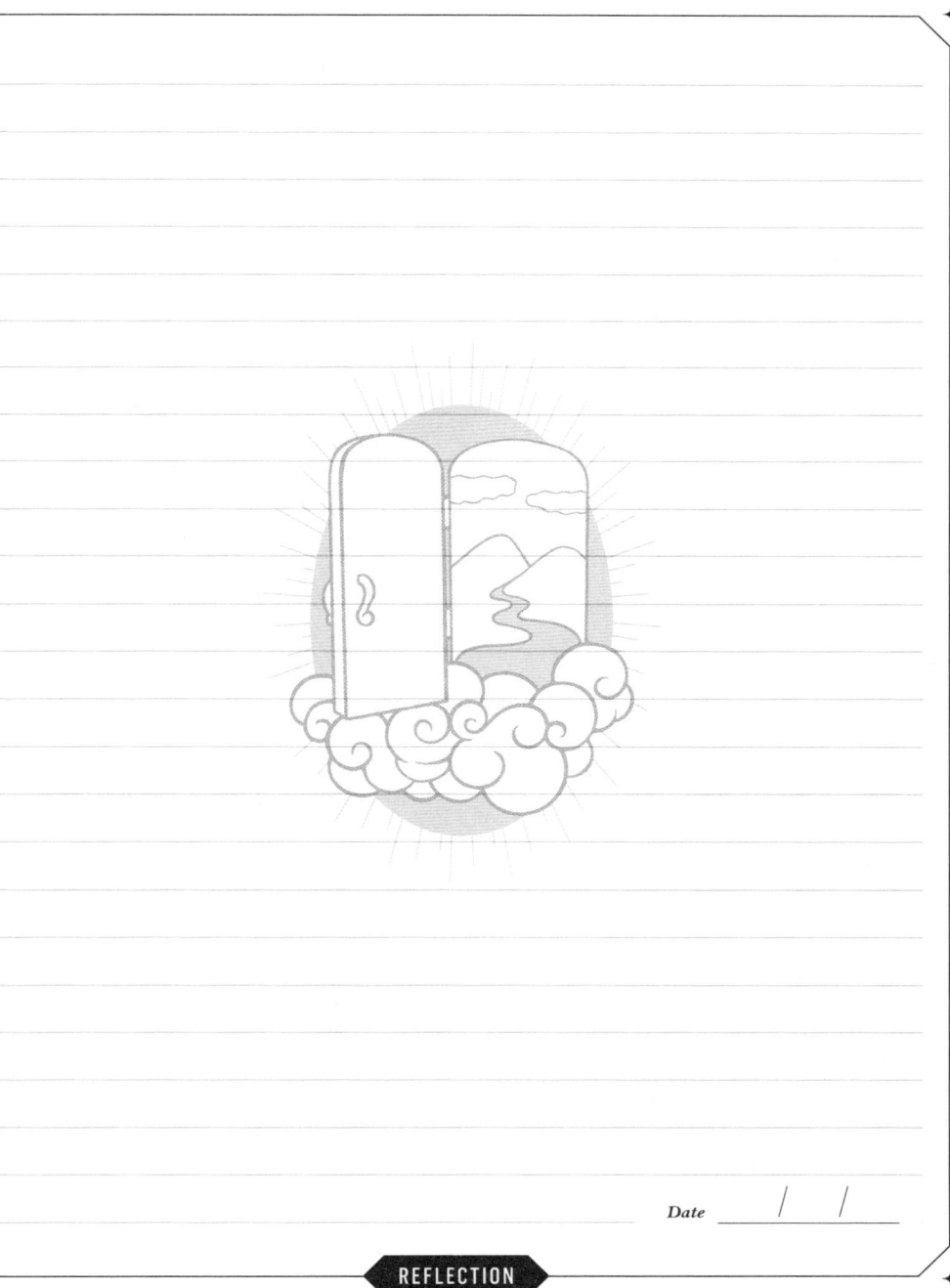

WHICH OF MY UNFULFILLED DREAMS IS STILL IMPORTANT? WHY HAVEN'T I ADDRESSED OR FULFILLED IT YET?

Date ___ / ___ / ___

Date _____ / _____ / _____

HOW CAN I BEST UTILIZE MY ENERGY?

Date ___/___/___

Date ___ / ___ / ___

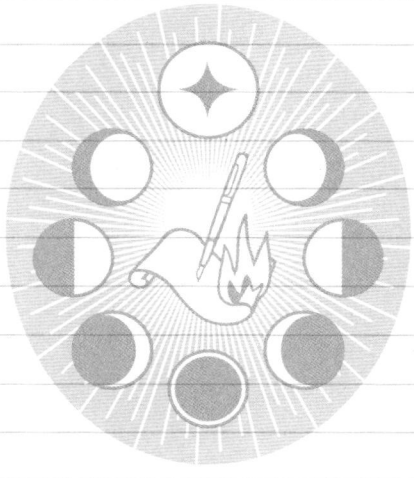

WHAT CHILDHOOD MEMORY HAS LEFT A NEGATIVE IMPRESSION ON ME, AND HOW IS IT CURRENTLY IMPACTING ME?

Date _____ / _____ / _____

Date _____ / ___ / ___

WHAT IS PREVENTING ME FROM BREAKING MY WORST
OR MOST UNWANTED HABIT?

Date _____ / _____ / _____

Date ___ / ___ / ___

WHAT LESSON HAVE I LEARNED THAT I CAN USE TO BETTER MYSELF?

Date _____ / _____ / _____

Date _____ / _____ / _____

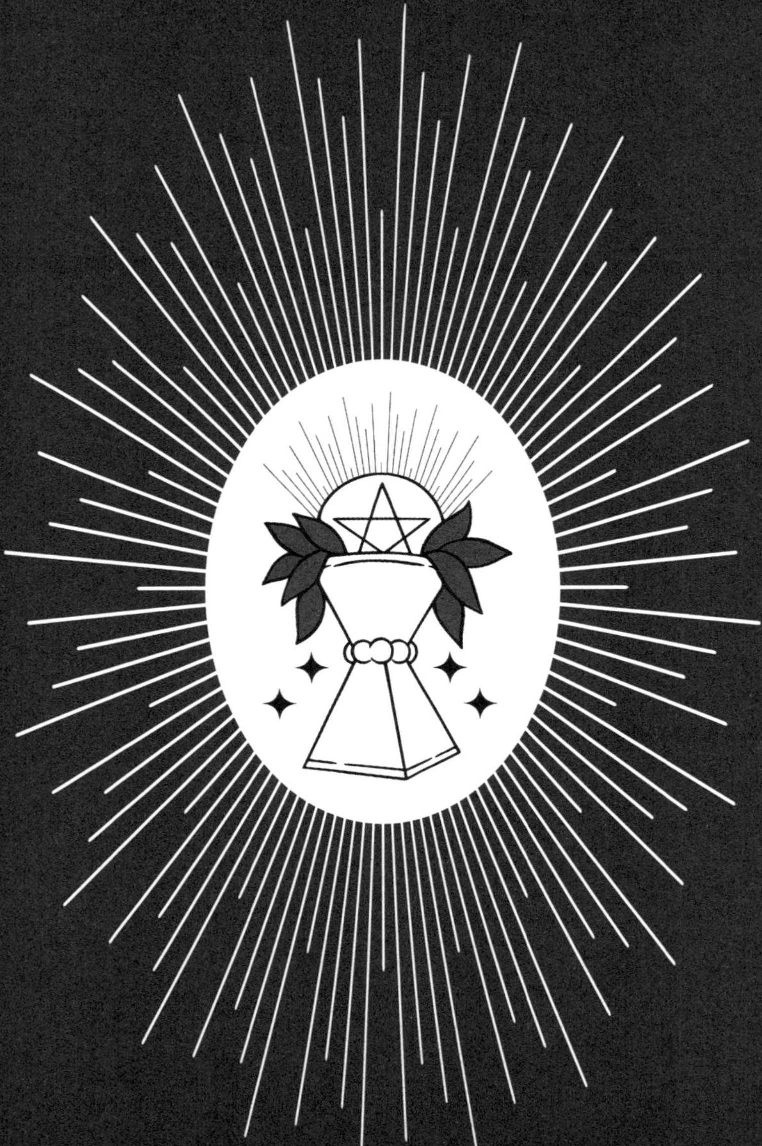

SAFE AND SEEN

✦

*I am tapping into my instincts and my emotions.
I can show my strength and don't have to hide from the
world like a crab in a shell. I am safe as I maneuver
through my environment. I am becoming a restored version
of myself as I tap into my intuition. I am protected and
continue to move forward toward my goals.*

HOW CAN I REACT DIFFERENTLY WHEN ATTACKED?

Date _____ / _____ / _____

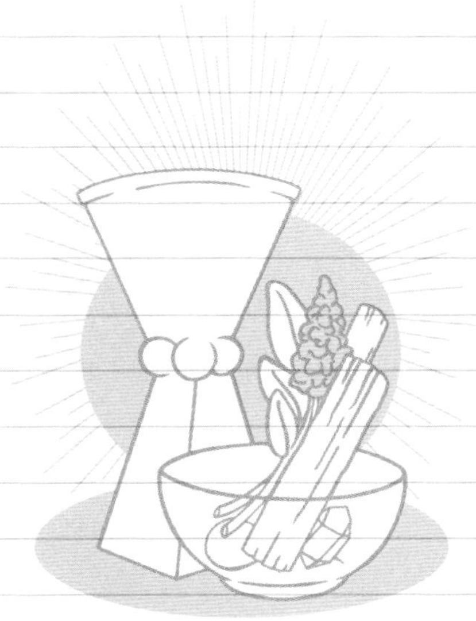

Date / /

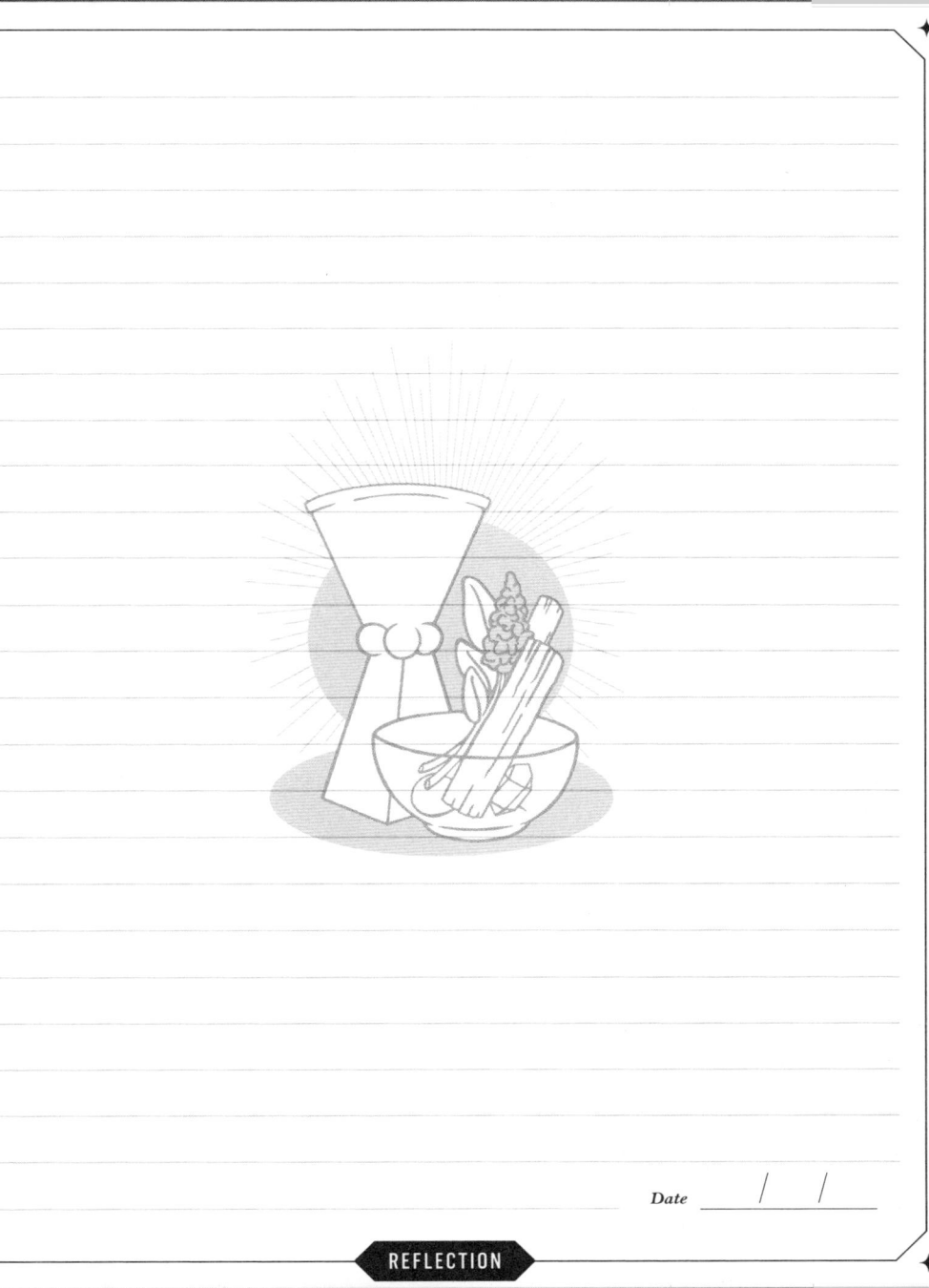

WHAT DO I NEED TO FORGIVE MYSELF FOR?

Date _____ / _____ / _____

Date _____ / _____ / _____

WHAT WOULD MY IDEAL DAY-TO-DAY SCHEDULE LOOK LIKE?
WHAT FIRST STEP CAN I TAKE TOWARD MAKING THAT A REALITY?

Date ___/___/___

Date _____ / _____ / _____

WHAT SIGNS HAVE I RECEIVED, AND HOW HAVE THEY GUIDED MY ACTIONS?

Date ___/___/___

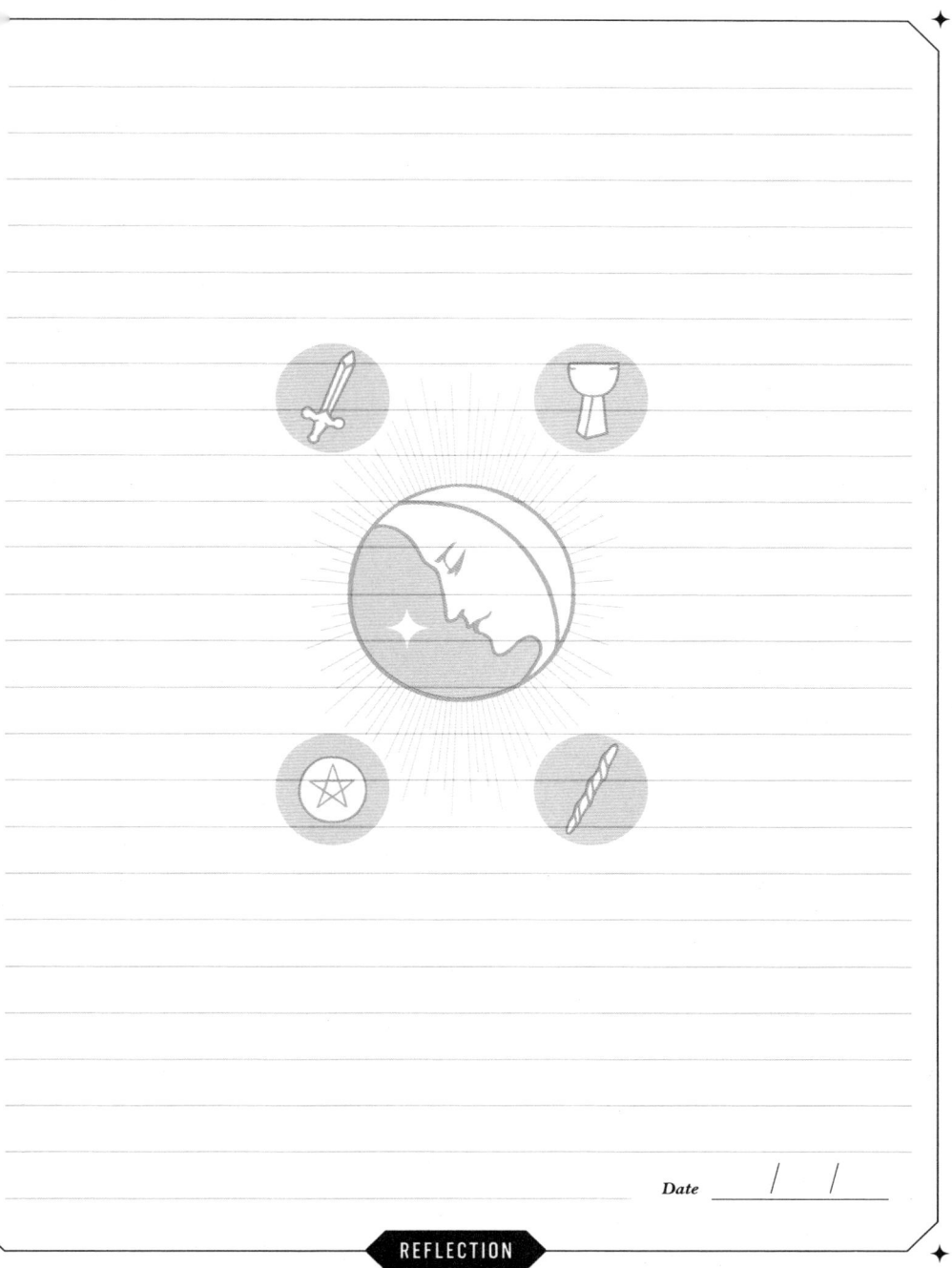

Date ___/___/___

WHO DO I NEED TO FORGIVE AND WHY?

Date _____ / _____ / _____

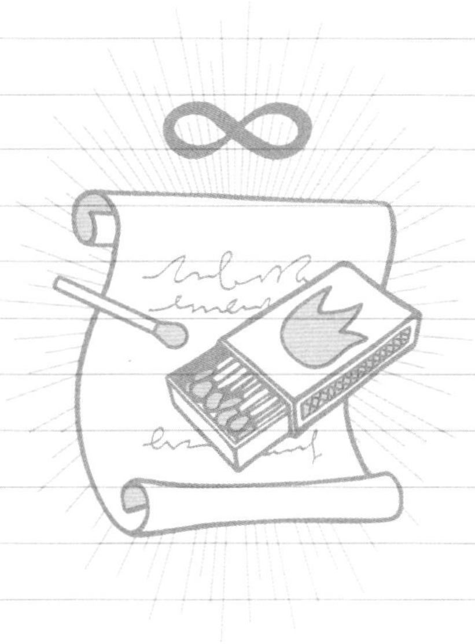

Date ____ / ____ / ____

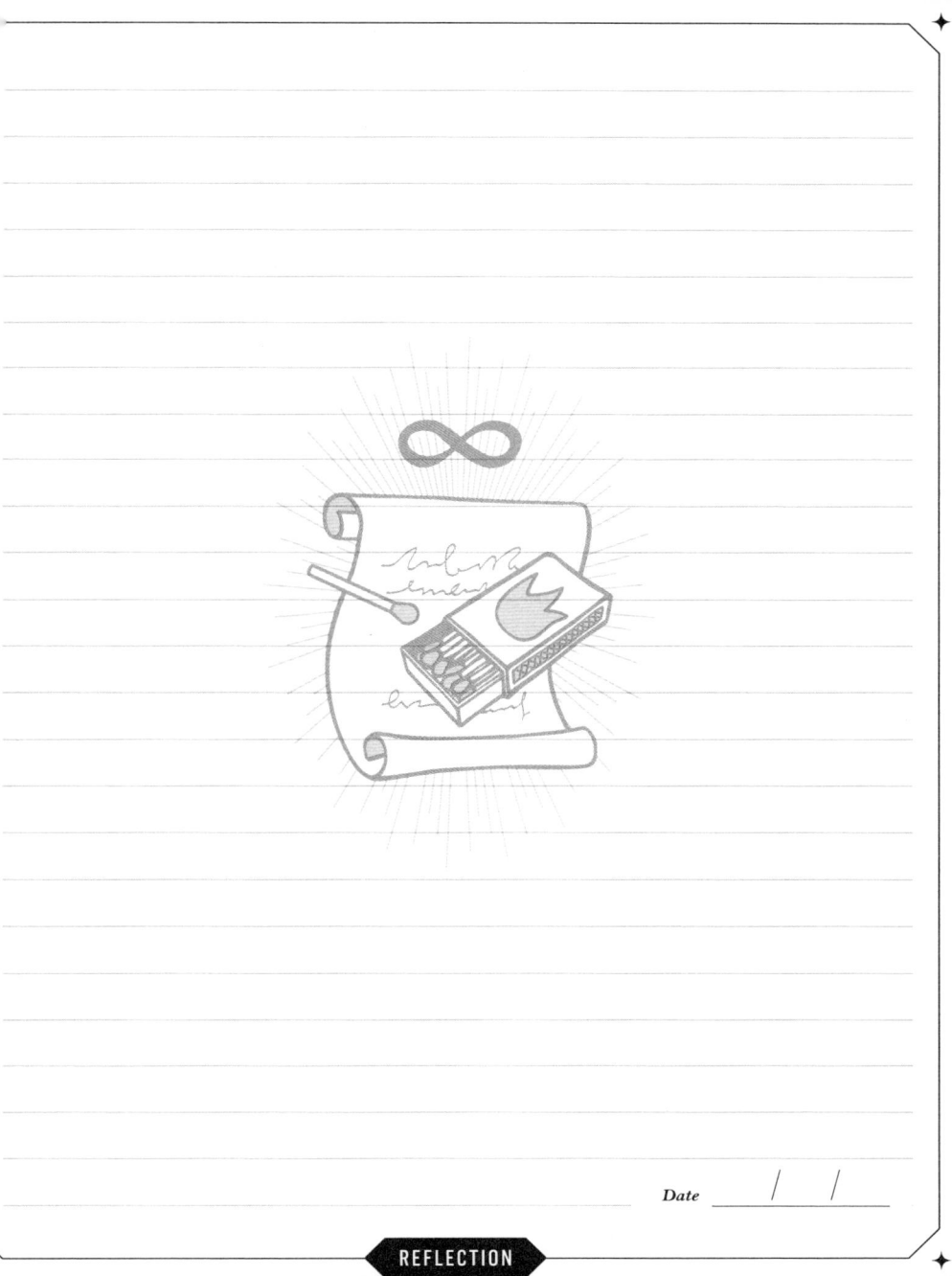

WHEN I'M NOT VIEWING MY LIFE THROUGH THE EYES OF OTHERS, HOW DO I ACTUALLY FEEL ABOUT IT?

Date ___/___/___

Date / /

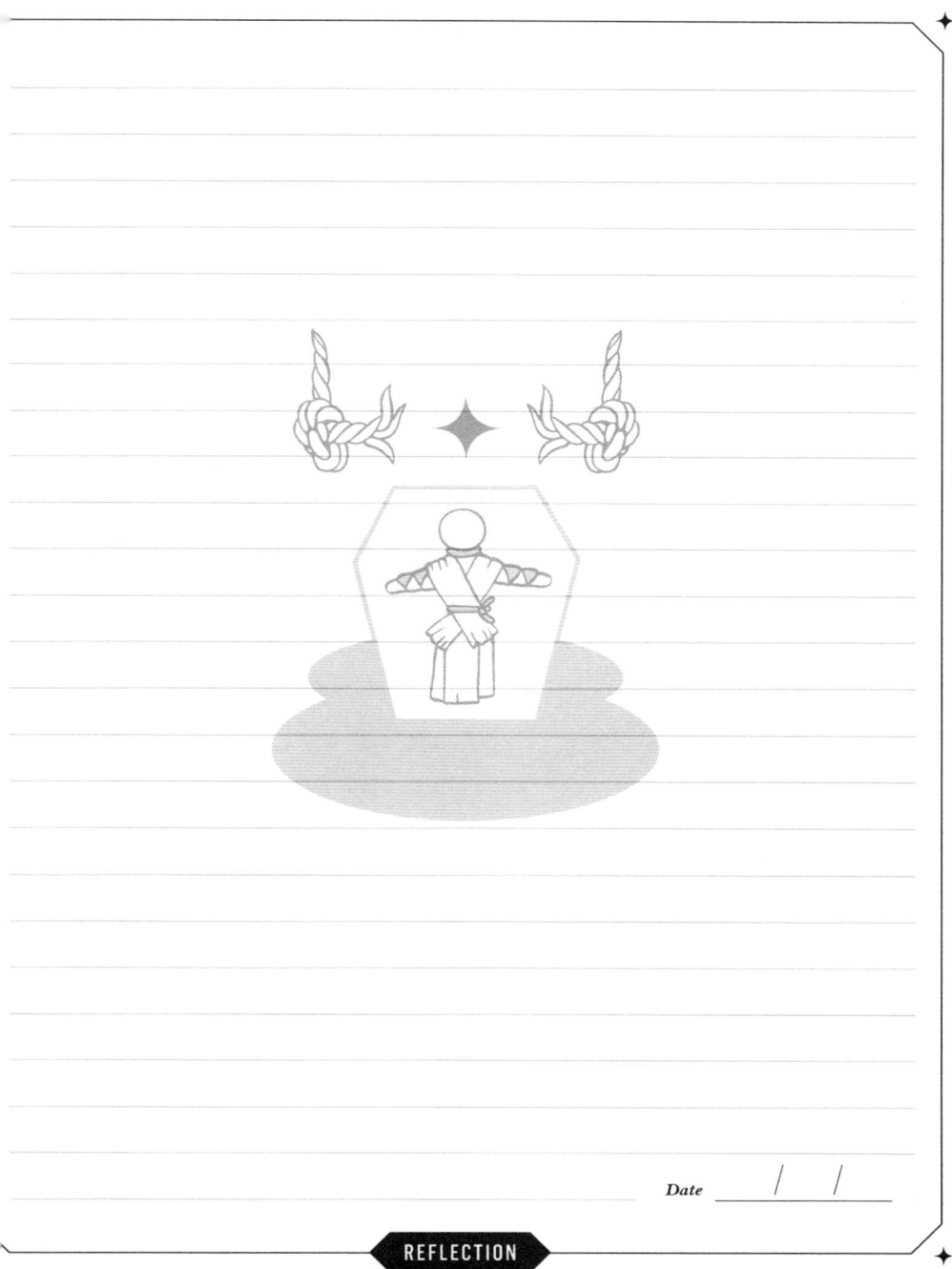

DO I FEEL LIKE I'M MOVING IN THE RIGHT DIRECTION? WHAT CAN I DO DIFFERENTLY OR WHAT SHOULD I KEEP DOING TO MOVE IN THE RIGHT DIRECTION?

Date ___ / ___ / ___

Date ___/___/___

WHAT MAKES ME FEEL MOST WHOLE?

Date ___/___/___

Date _____ / _____ / _____

AM I HOLDING ON TO ANYTHING UNNECESSARY?
IF SO, WHAT AND WHY?

Date ___/___/___

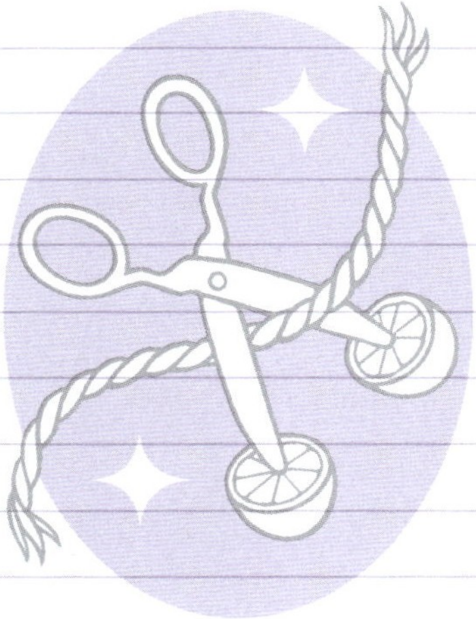

Date / /

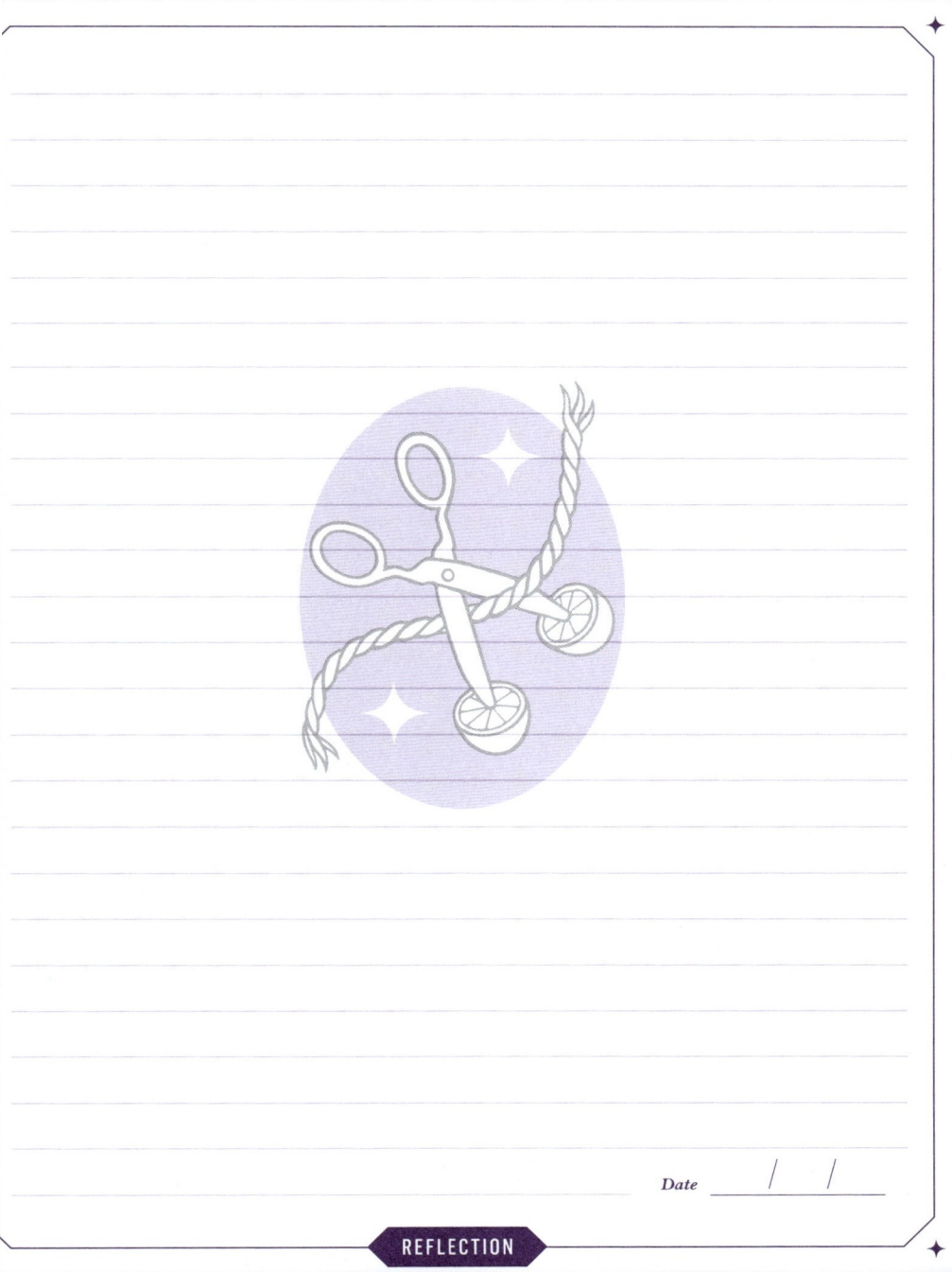

AM I USING MY TIME AND ENERGY WISELY?
IF NOT, WHAT SHIFTS CAN I MAKE?

Date _____ / _____ / _____

Date ___ / ___ / ___

WHAT BRINGS ME PEACE, AND WHAT DOES THAT FEEL LIKE IN MY BODY?

Date _____ / _____ / _____

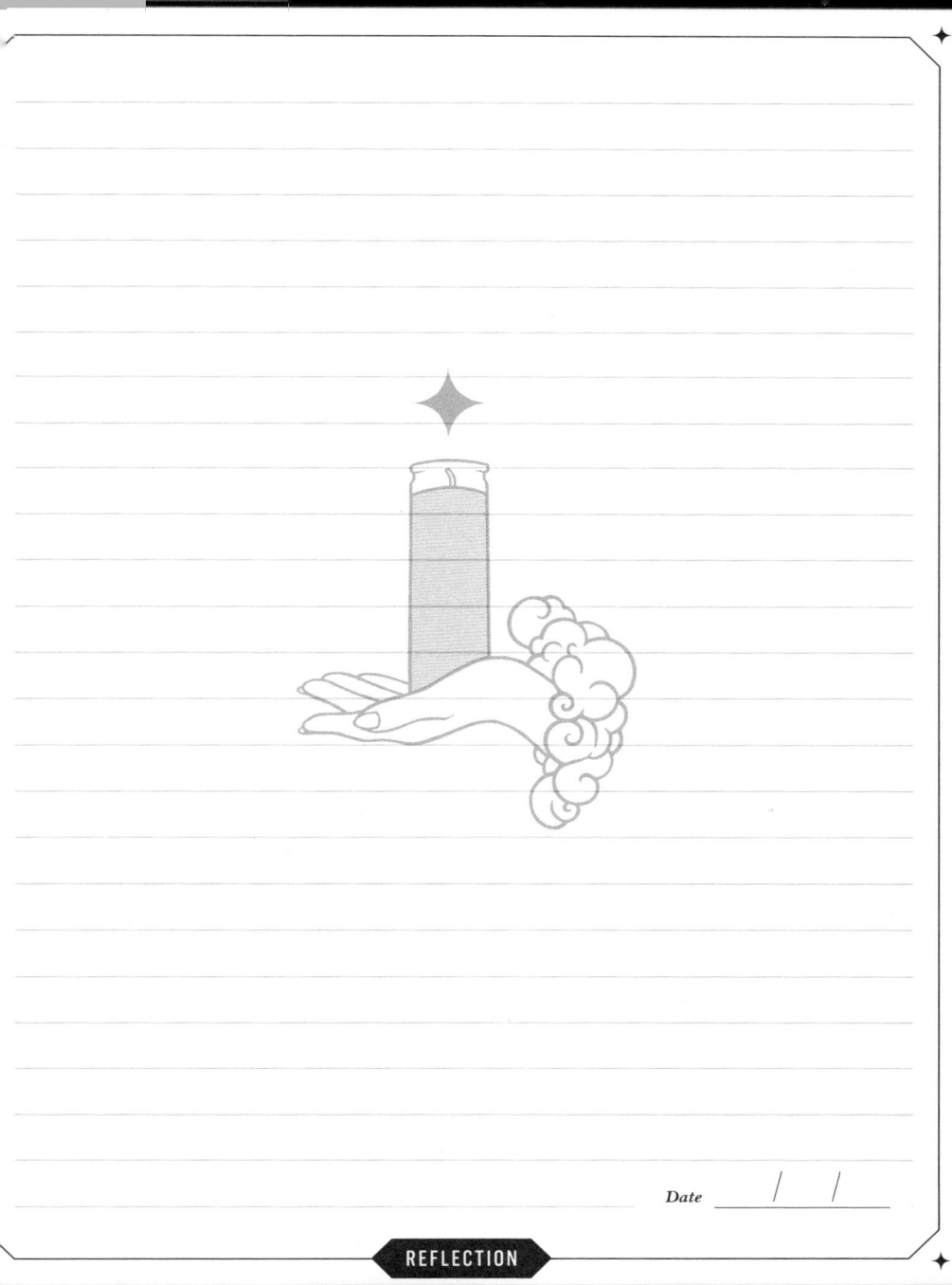

Date _____ / _____ / _____

WHAT SAPPED ME OF MY ENERGY TODAY?

Date _____ / _____ / _____

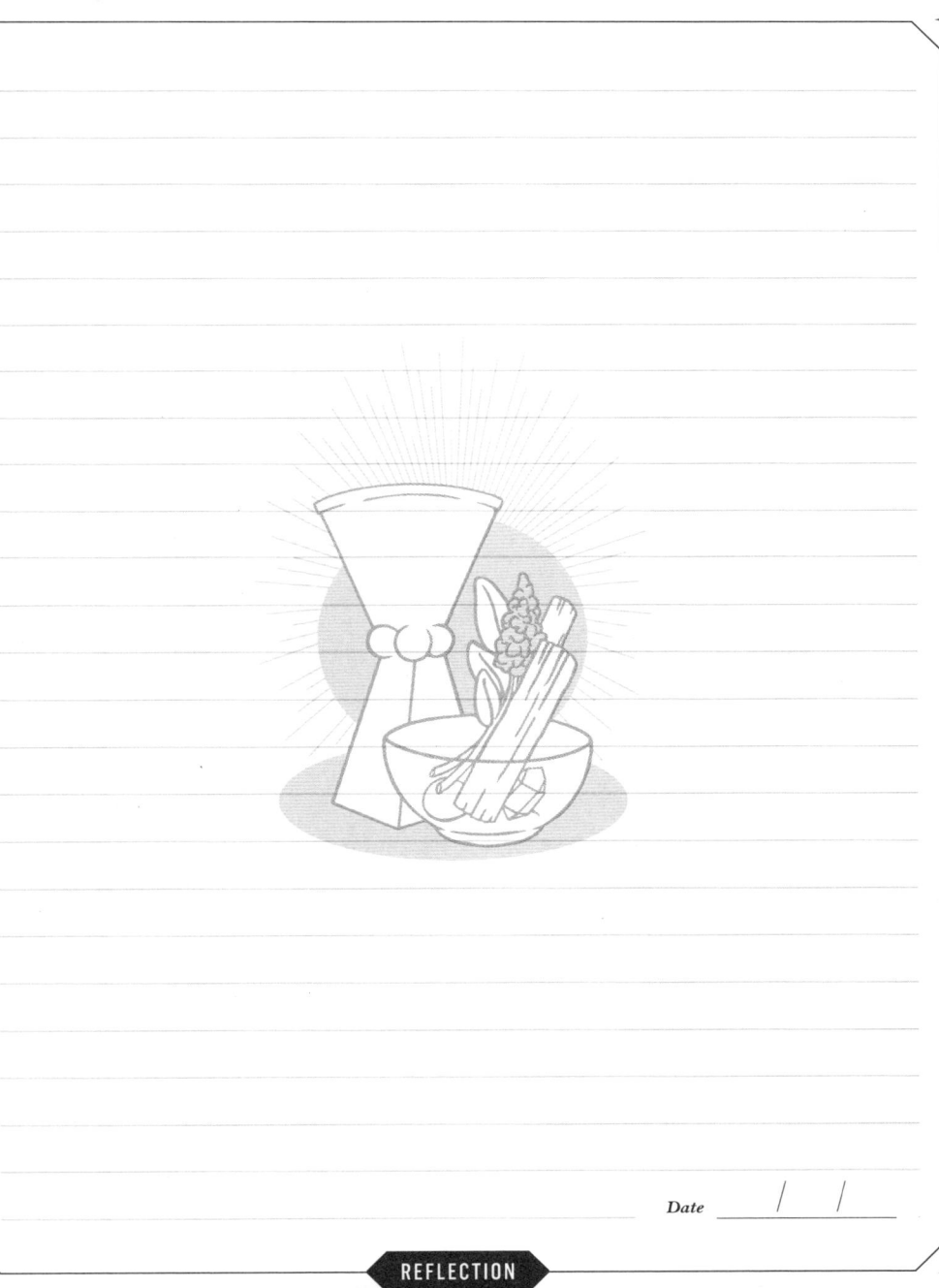

Date ___/___/___

WHAT IS MY HIGHEST PURPOSE OR CALLING IN THIS LIFE?

Date _____ / _____ / _____

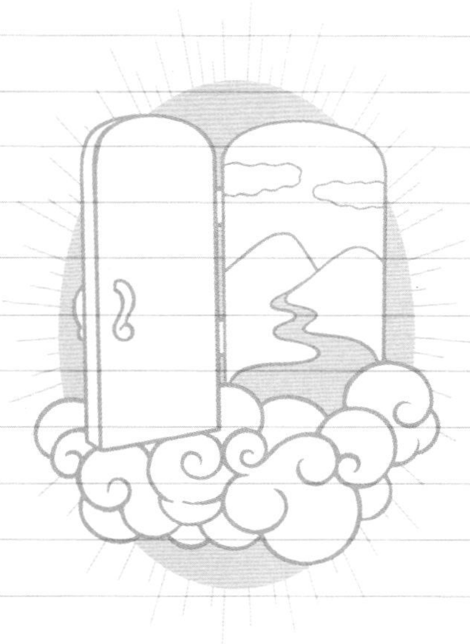

Date ___ / ___ / ___

REFLECTION

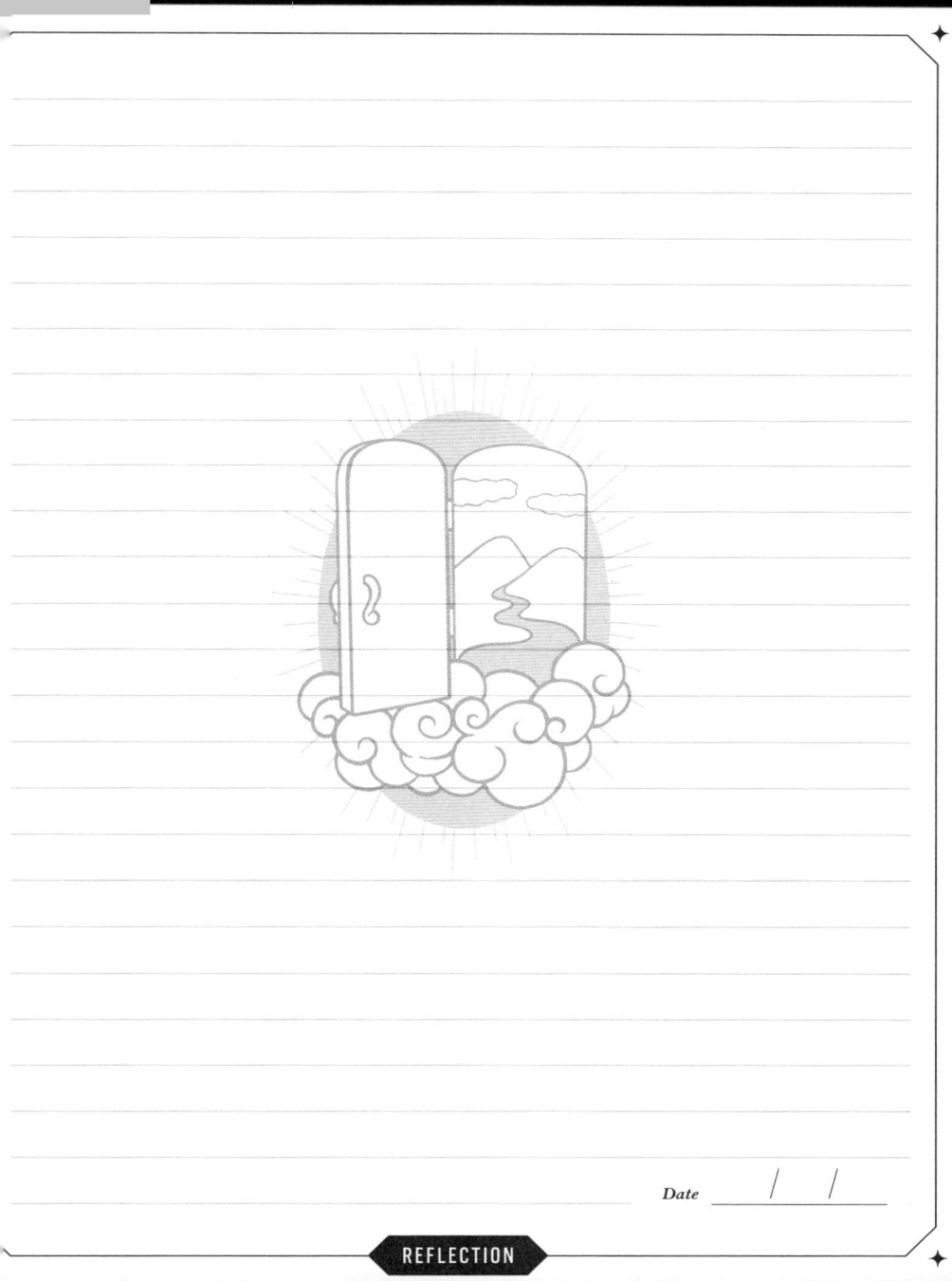

WHAT GOAL WOULD I LIKE TO ACCOMPLISH? HOW QUICKLY CAN I ACCOMPLISH IT, AND WHAT STEPS CAN I TAKE TO GET THERE?

Date ___ / ___ / ___

Date _____ / _____ / _____

WHAT AM I READY TO BRING INTO MY LIFE?

Date _____ / _____ / _____

Date _____ / _____ / _____

I am

My life is m,

as I paint it, I sh

of a new, ref

artist.

canvas and,

the old in favor

shed palette.

WHAT WORK HAVE I DONE TO BE A BETTER VERSION OF MYSELF?

Date _____ / _____ / _____

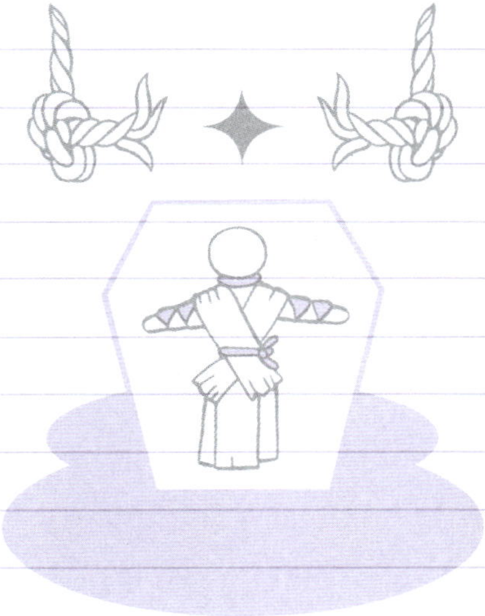

Date / /

IN WHAT WAYS CAN I COMMUNICATE MY EMOTIONS MORE EFFECTIVELY?

Date _____ / ___ / ___

Date _____ / _____ / _____

WHAT MAKES ME REACT DEFENSIVELY? WHY?

Date _____ / _____ / _____

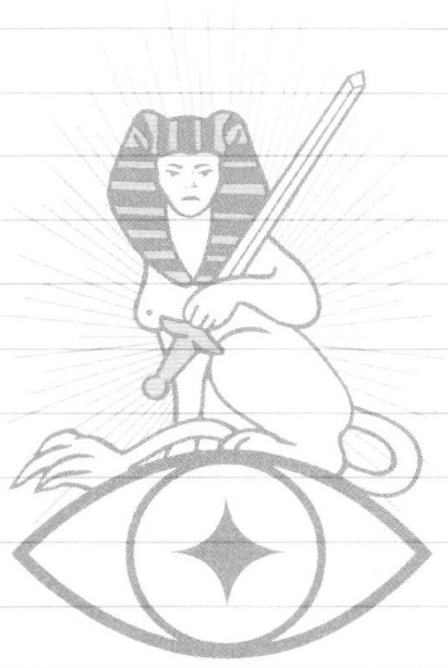

Date / /

WHAT MAKES ME PROCRASTINATE ON THINGS I NEED TO GET DONE?

Date ___/___/___

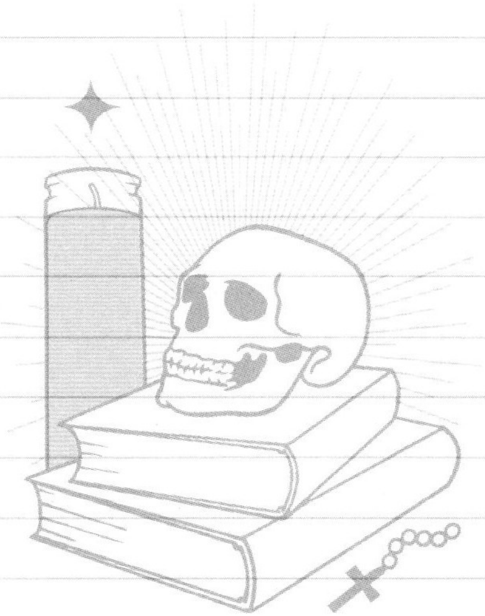

Date / /

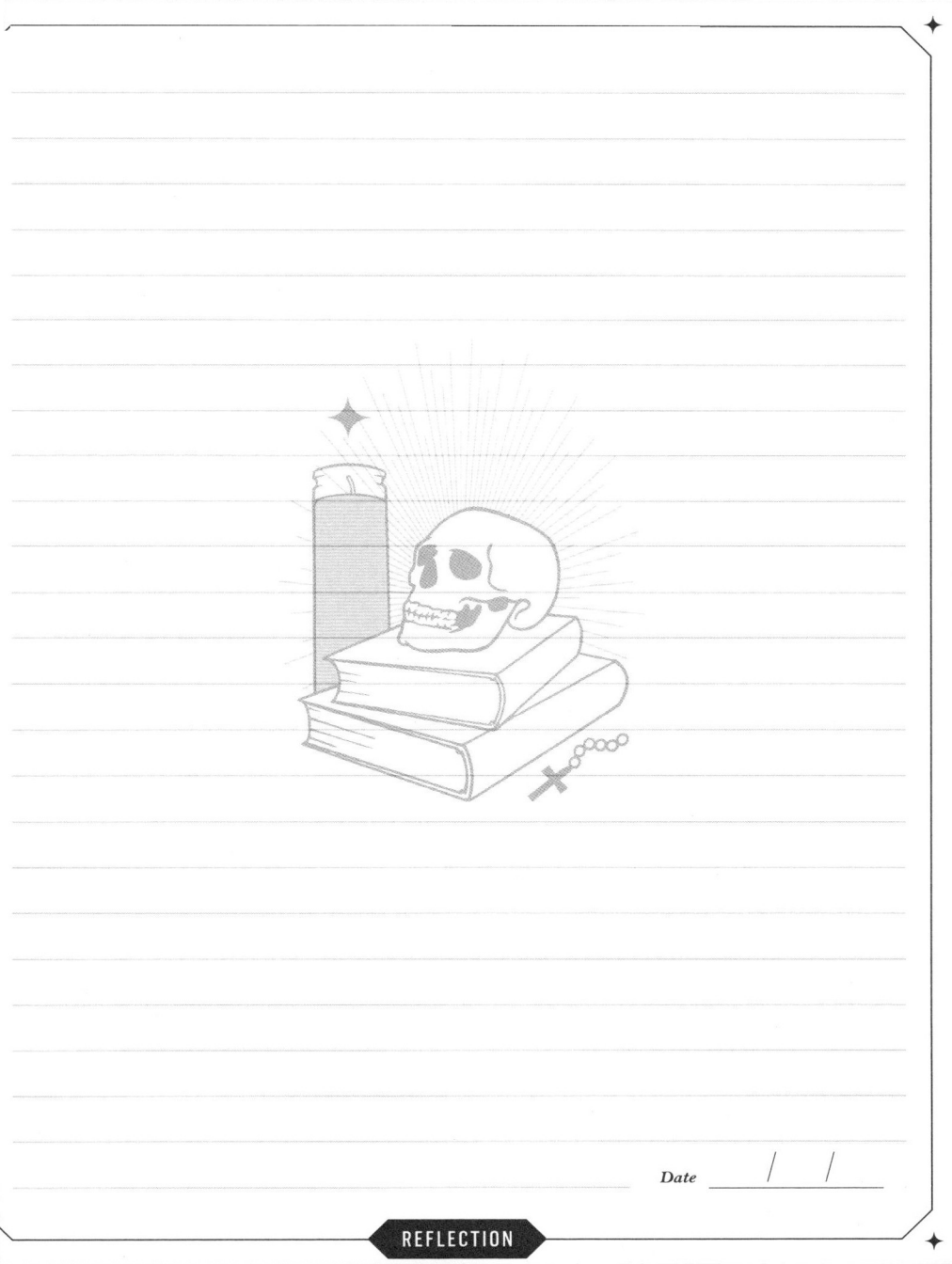

WHAT OBSTACLES DO I NEED TO REMOVE TO GET WHERE I WANT TO BE?

Date ___ / ___ / ___

Date ___ / ___ / ___

WHAT CAN I DO TO BRING CLARITY WHEN I FEEL CONFUSED?

Date _____ / _____ / _____

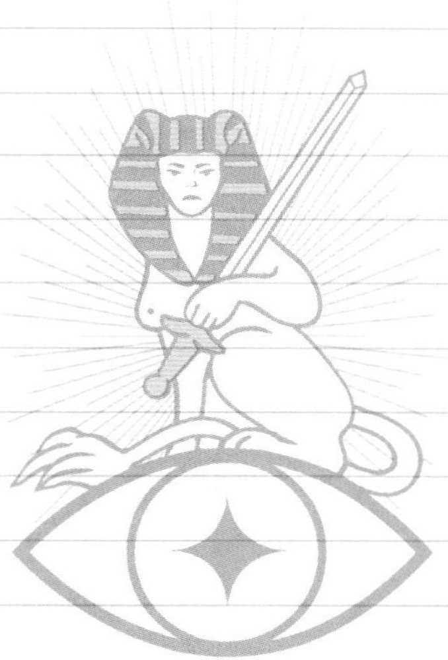

Date ___ / ___ / ___

I am ready t

behind me s

into my power

source to creat

leave my past

that I can step

nd use it as a

my own future.

HOW CAN I HELP MYSELF THROUGH DEPRESSION AND ANXIETY?

Date / /

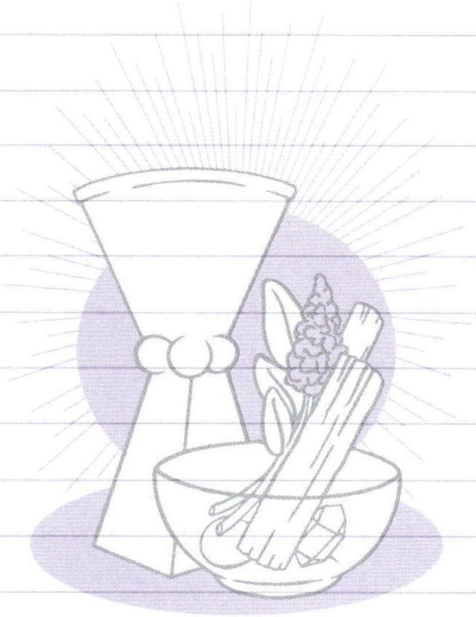

Date / /

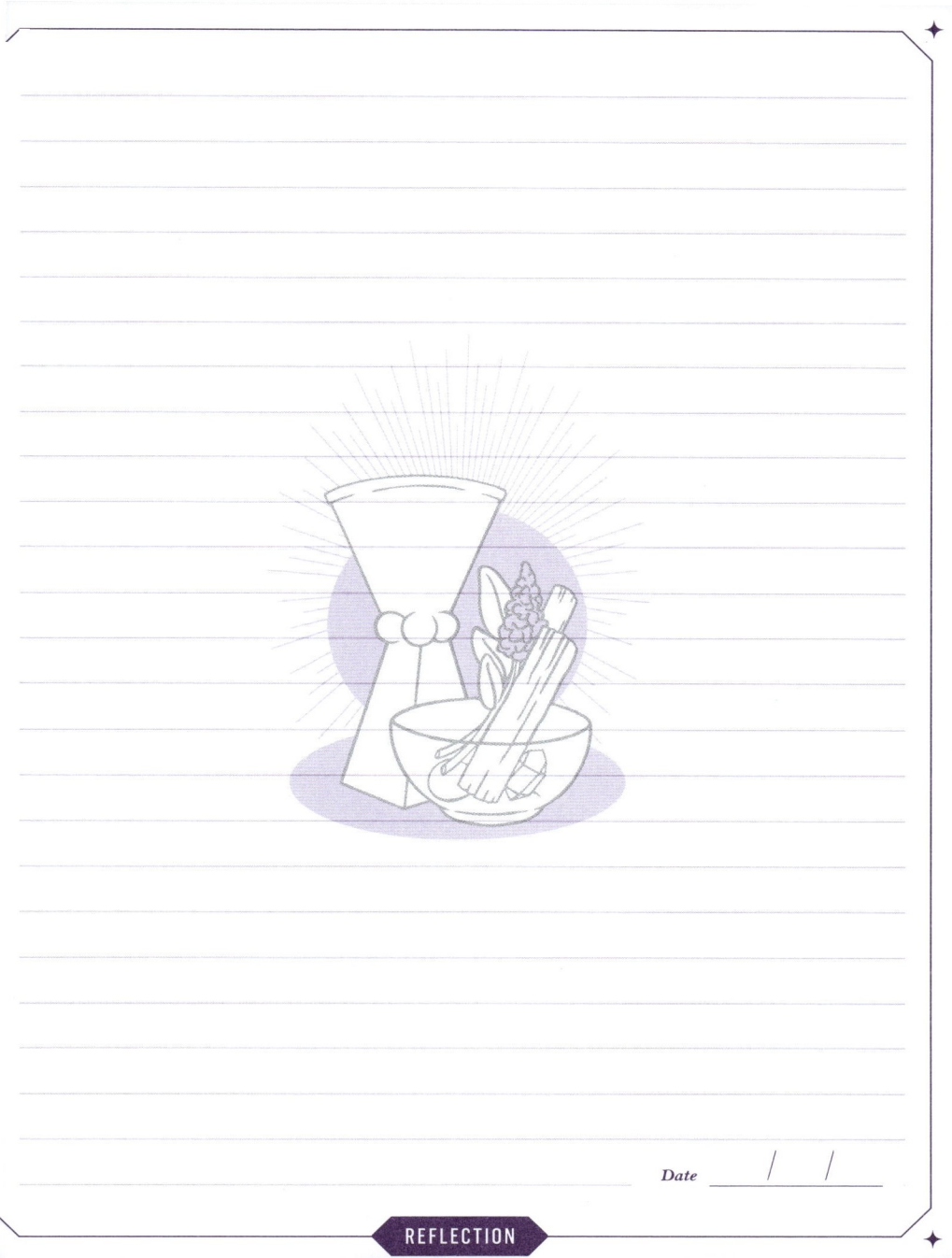

IN WHAT WAYS DO I FEEL LOVE? IN WHAT WAYS DO I NOT FEEL LOVE?

Date ___/___/___

Date _____ / _____ / _____

WHAT RELATIONSHIP IN MY LIFE IS CURRENTLY ACTING AS A MIRROR TO TEACH ME SOMETHING?

Date _____ / _____ / _____

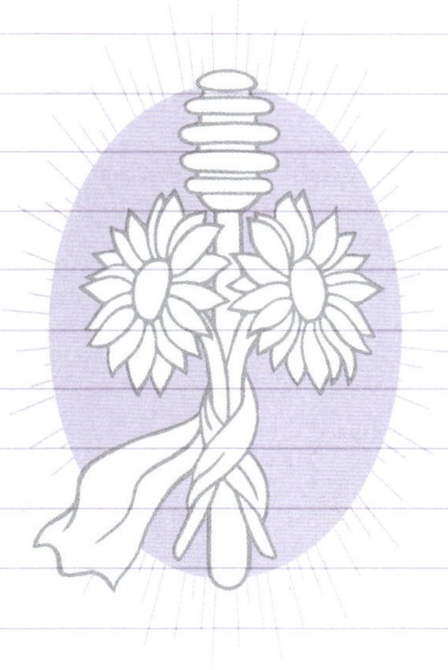

Date ____ / ____ / ____

WHAT PERSONAL ACCOMPLISHMENT AM I MOST PROUD OF?

Date ___ / ___ / ___

Date ___ / ___ / ___

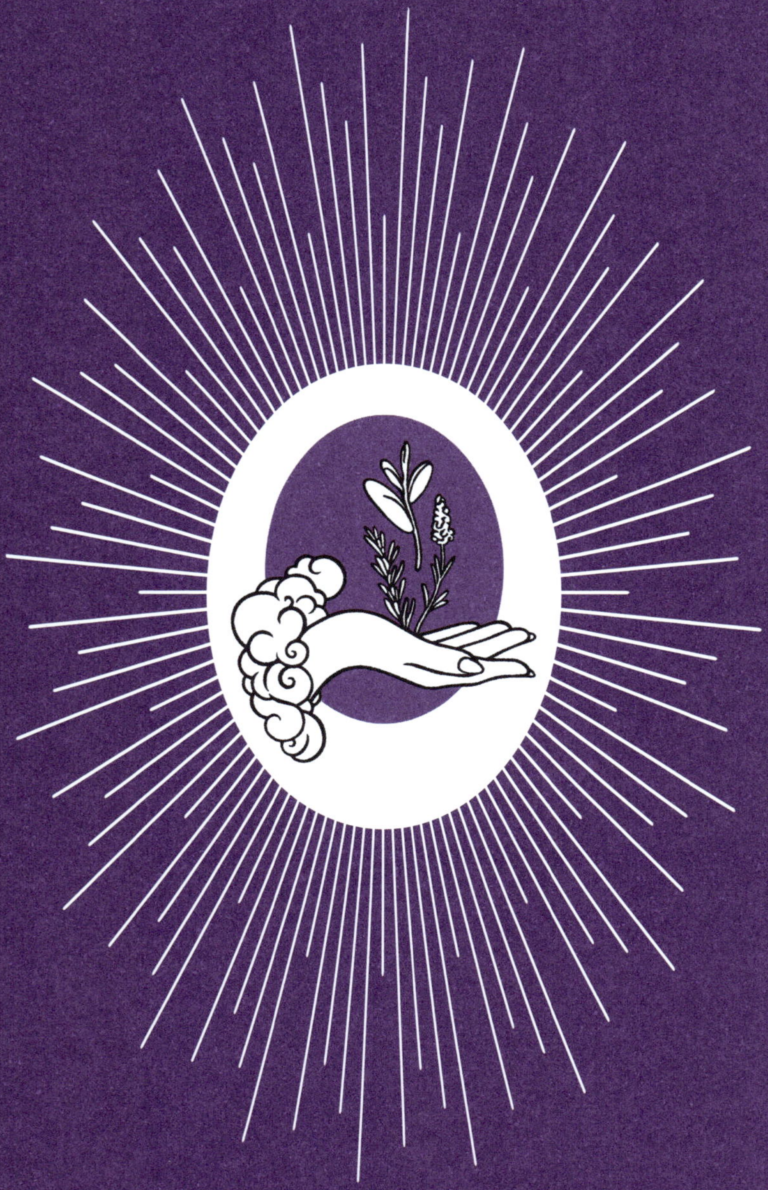

THE INNER POWER PRAYER

✦

I am liberated from preconceived notions, old habits,
and stale relationships. I welcome change for growth to new
dimensions. I tune into the universe, knowing that signs
will surely come my way. A new, more evolved version of my
highest self is blooming as I unleash my inner power.

You've come to the last page of the journal. Have you finished your journey? If you feel like you still want to respond to and reflect on the prompts, flip to a different page. If you feel like you've completed this journey, flip back to the first question you answered in this journal.

WHAT DO YOU WISH YOU COULD SAY TO
THAT VERSION OF YOURSELF?

CLARKSON POTTER is a trademark and POTTER with colophon is a registered trademark of Penguin Random House LLC.

This work is based on *Your Intuition Led You Here* (Rodale Books, 2021).

ISBN 978-0-593-13954-7

Printed in China

Editor: Deanne Katz
Illustrations: Valentina Zapata
Designer: Amy Sly, The Sly Studio
Production editor: Abby Oladipo
Production manager: Kelli Tokos
Marketer: Chloe Aryeh

10 9 8 7 6 5 4 3 2 1

First Edition